PRAISE

BE YOUR SELF

D0728606

"*Be Yourself and Be Well* is a must read to take control of your life and live your dream, a clear and concise guide to healing from a soul level. Dr Hiebert masterfully teaches the art and experience of mindfulness to reduce inflammation, pain, aging and anxiety while improving relationships with yourself and others. Dr Hiebert's practices are profound and simple, bringing the essence of self healing into every aspect of your life."

—JUDY GRIFFIN, PhD, AUTHOR OF *MOTHER NATURE'S HERBAL* AND *FLOWERS THAT HEAL*

"When I met Steven twenty years ago, I was deeply touched by his expertise and intuitive talents, along with his tremendous compassion and empathy. This book is a sharing of a very deep wisdom that comes from what he has learned over these years. I believe you will find yourself changed and a happier and healthier person when you've completed this book. I know it has done this for me!"

—STEPHEN G. HENKE, MD-BOARD-CERTIFIED FAMILY AND INTEGRATIVE MEDICINE PHYSICIAN

"This is an inspiring, soul-stirring book about health and wellness that will not only ignite one's passion for living but put it into everyday motion."

—DEANNA MINICH, PhD, AUTHOR OF *WHOLE DETOX*

"I have implemented Steven's easy-to-understand philosophies when meeting with my yoga students who are looking for a deeper purpose. The healing exercises invite students to take a closer look at their inner selves and take up a confident 'I can' attitude. It's not just a one-time read; as it can be reread and applied many times over. It's the perfect tune-up for anyone seeking connection to their true Self."

—KATE ROBERTSON, RYT 200 YOGA INSTRUCTOR AND AUTHOR OF *IMMIGRATION: WHAT NO POLITICIAN WILL TELL YOU*

BE YOUR SELF

BE WELL

CONNECTING WITH YOUR
SOUL'S POWER TO HEAL

DR. STEVEN HIEBERT

ISBN 13: 978-1-36489-065-6

Printed in the United States of America
First Printing: 2017
21 20 19 18 17   5 4 3 2 1

Cover and interior design by Ryan Scheife, Mayfly Design

Minneapolis, MN
www.wiseinkpub.com

To order, visit www.itascabooks.com or call 1-800-901-3480.
Reseller discounts available.

CONTENTS

INTRODUCTION

HEALING IS IN MY BLOOD. FOR ME, THERE'S NOTHing else like it. I rarely feel more alive and joyful than when I'm working. It's not a job at all. It's a calling. I've discovered some wonderful, life-changing things along the way. I want to pass along some of what I've learned in hopes that it will help you live a more joyful, passionate life too.

Whether they know it or not, my clients are my teachers. Each and every one has something important to teach me, some incredible new gift to share. More than anything else, my clients have shown me the incredible resilience and tenacity of the human spirit. It is limitless.

I have witnessed so many instances of incredible healing, healing that was unexpected and sometimes unexplainable. What I want you to know is that you can do the same thing. You can heal. I have complete faith in you. Access the power of your own spirit, and you can overcome anything.

My father and uncle were chiropractors. My great-grandfather was a countryside healer that people sought out for help with their ailments.

I've followed a similar path and have been a holistically minded chiropractor and healer for more than twenty-five years.

Over the years, I have used just about every therapy you can think of, short of drugs and surgery. I have given diets and nutritional supplements of all kinds. I have used flower essences, essential oils, and homeopathy. I have adjusted just about every bone in the human body. I've done work on ligaments, tendons, fasciae, and muscle. I've pushed on trigger points and acupuncture points. Detoxification, fasting, juicing—you name it and I've done it.

But something has gradually become so clear it's undeniable. The power of your own spirit is what makes healing possible. It's not what I do. It's who you are that matters most.

Spirituality is the best medicine there is. Unfortunately, it is grossly underutilized and all too often completely neglected. Instead of being a complement to physical medicine, spirituality or energy medicine needs to be the primary approach.

This isn't anything new. I am simply today's messenger for a timeless and universal truth. People like Rumi, for example, were writing about it hundreds of years ago.

This book is not meant to be read in one sitting. Take your time and allow things to steep and take root before moving on. Take the time to do the healing exercises at the end of each chapter. You'll get the most out of it if you are an active reader. You can read, learn, and heal all at the same time.

Speaking of the healing exercises, you will need to use a journal or notebook while you work through this book. If you have one lying around, dig it out and repurpose it. Otherwise, you can purchase one. It doesn't need to be fancy. Simple is good.

Healing isn't something you do in a day. It takes commitment and the willingness to make it a daily practice. It unfolds over a lifetime. Read a chapter. Do the healing exercise. Write about your experience. Then wait. The next time you pick up the book, ask your Self if you're ready to read the next chapter or if you need to review the prior chapter and do the exercise again. Move on when you feel ready.

Another thing to keep in mind is that you can do the exercises many times. Each time, you will discover something new—a new awareness or insight will come to you. I've been doing these exercises daily for many years and I continue to make new discoveries about my Self. I expect you will too.

I am so glad you've decided to read this book. Thank you from the bottom of my heart.

BE YOUR SELF AND BE WELL!

CHAPTER ONE

HEALING IS SPIRITUAL

"The next big frontier in medicine is energy medicine."
— DR. OZ

HAVE YOU GIVEN MUCH THOUGHT TO HEALING; what it is and how it happens?

Like most people, I took healing for granted. It was something that happened automatically after I got sick or injured. If I rested and gave it a little time, I got better. That was it. Healing was bandaging a wound or eating chicken soup. It certainly didn't have anything to do with energy or spirituality.

Then one day a former colleague offered to help me using what she called an "energy healing." She instructed me to lie down. Then she stood quietly next to me and gently put her hands on me. If you had been there, that is all you would have seen her do.

She told me to be calm and breathe deeply. As she held her warm hands on my body, I responded in ways that I found surprising. There was a warm, almost buzzing sensation going through me. My arms and hands gradually moved into different positions like they had lives of their own.

I simultaneously felt like an observer and participant. It was all very strange and unusual. I had never experienced anything quite like it.

I found my Self wanting to move in ways I couldn't explain. It didn't make sense to me, but I found I could relax and go with it.

I let my body move the way it wanted to move. If I felt like making sounds, I did.

Eventually my hands clenched up in a way that reminded me of a person with cerebral palsy. The muscle contractions were so strong that I wondered if I was going to unclench after the healing was done.

The contractions did stop. My arms and hands returned to normal. All the sensations diminished and I felt surprisingly calm and relaxed. My colleague said the healing was done and I could get up.

At that time in my life I had a food allergy or sensitivity to cow's milk. If I consumed even the smallest amount of any dairy product, I got sick. I got headaches and had trouble thinking and focusing. It made me feel very tired and out of it. Those things bothered me so much that I was very careful to avoid dairy products altogether.

After the healing, I told another colleague about my experience. He said he wouldn't be surprised if it changed my food allergy. I thought, "What? No way!"

But he was insistent and I was intrigued. So I went out with my colleagues and, expecting I was going to suffer for it, ate pizza. Amazingly, I had no symptoms whatsoever. In a period of a few hours I went from getting sick after eating cheese, to having no reaction at all.

At the time, I had no idea what happened. I certainly couldn't explain it. But being able to eat cheese without getting sick was miraculous.

Nothing physical had been done do me. I didn't take any pills or have a surgery. There was no logical reason for my suddenly being able to eat cheese without getting sick. But the truth is, something profound happened, and I could.

I needed to know what it was. But figuring that out took a lot longer than I thought it would. It has taken the accumulated experiences of many years to show me what took place. In the end, it is shockingly simple, yet can be surprisingly difficult to pull off.

What I know today is that I responded to my colleague's gentle touch. I came forward, and the energy of my spirit changed and healed my body.

That experience was the beginning of the revolution that has completely changed my way of living and being. It has resulted in fundamental changes in the way I see health and healing. It has dramatically altered the way I work with others.

Back then, I thought my colleague healed me. I lived under the assumption that helping professionals were the healers, that the healers and their techniques made the healing happen.

What I have discovered is that I was the source of my own healing. She was just a helper. She happened to be a very good helper. But the truth is, she helped me heal. I am the one who created the healing.

I want you to know that you can do the same thing. You were born with the power to heal. It's right there inside of you. You might need a little help. But with the right help, you can heal.

I have been in practice for more than twenty-five years. I have used many different tools and techniques during that time.

I have adjusted almost every part of the human skeleton. I have used massage and trigger point therapy. I have given people herbs and vitamins. I have used flower essences, essential oils, and homeopathy. I have recommended diets. These are all good and useful tools. And they are all things I do to my clients.

The truth of the matter is things generally won't change very much if it's just me doing things to you. What I've seen over and over again is that if you aren't an active participant, it doesn't matter what I do. I won't be able to help you. You are the one with the power to heal, not me. No medicine has the power to make up for your absence. But if I can help you discover that you have the power to heal, anything is possible.

Real and powerful healing originates in the realm of spirit. Your spirit is where the power to heal comes from. And because there is nothing that spirit cannot do, there is nothing that your spirit cannot heal. Access the power of your spiritual presence and you can heal almost anything.

The truth is, you are a spiritual being. Spirituality is the air you breathe and the food you eat. As a spiritual being, you are the source of your own health and well-being. Your body responds to you and follows where you lead.

True healing—the healing that has the power to change everything about you and your life—is recovering and expressing the essence of who you are. It is returning to your awareness of, and the ability to freely express, your true Self.

You live in a physical, human body, but that body isn't who you are. You're far more than the body you live in. You are the inside. You are the life force. You are the unseen, the inner spiritual entity that was created by the divine. You are powerful.

Another way to think about this is that you are the life force that makes your body a living organism. You are so important that without you, your body would die. You are, quite literally, the source for the life and health of your body.

When you are fully present, your body will respond to the energy you provide. It will use your life force to create physical strength and health.

I see the effects of my spiritual presence or absence in my own life. When I'm present and aware of who I am, things are good. I feel strong, happy, and healthy.

But when I lose my Self, I make bad choices, things go poorly, and I start to get sick.

I have three children under ten. They make a lot of noise and big messes to go with it. But the way I respond is up to me. They might be noisy, but my response is not about them. It's about me.

When I'm present and centered, I respond with kindness and love. When I'm able to stay present and engaged, the noise doesn't bother me that much. I'm a calming presence.

But if I get too busy and lose touch with my Self, I get mad. I storm around and yell at them. I make the noise and chaos worse, not better.

It has very little to do with my children. It's all about me and my ability to stay present and be my Self.

The same is true for you. Your spiritual presence directly influences your own personal health and well-being and the health and well-being of everyone around you. Spiritual healing has the power to change your entire life. All you need to do is say yes to your Self. Healing is saying yes to your inner spirit and then bringing it to life through your physical form.

This is a book about healing. But reading about healing is not the same as healing. Healing is experiential. You must come forward, be your Self, and access the power of your inner spirit.

Healing is facilitated by the quiet inner listening that allows you to reconnect with your inner voice. It will guide you and tell you what to do.

It's something you must experience for your Self. I don't know what your personal experience will be. But I have no doubt you will know it when you feel it.

To help you with this process, I have included healing exercises at the end of each chapter. They will help you take what you've learned and integrate it into your life.

This book is a general guide that describes the common threads of healing. But while there are similarities in the healing journey, everyone's path is unique. The specifics of what you might need to do to heal can be very different from what someone else might need to do.

I cannot tell you exactly what you need to do. I can give you the general outline. I can describe the commonalities and general process. I can even tell you where it will end if you follow the path to its conclusion. But I cannot tell you exactly what to do.

You'll have to use what you have learned and allow your true Self to unwind and express as it will. Because, in the end, you are the healer you seek.

For most people, this is the beginning and not the end. Take what you've read and then bring it to life in your own way. When all is said and done, it is your ability to outwardly live who you are on the inside that matters most.

BE YOUR SELF AND BE WELL!

‖‖‖

HEALING EXERCISE

Seeing Your Self as a Spiritual Being

Find a quiet place where you can sit comfortably. The goal is to be calm and relaxed, undistracted and alert.

Once you are seated, close your eyes and focus on your breathing. Breathe deeply, slowly, and rhythmically for a few minutes.

I like to breathe in and out through my nose. Others prefer to breathe in through the nose and out through the mouth. Do whatever feels best to you.

Follow the air as it moves in and out of your body. Feel your chest rise and fall as you breathe, noticing how you feel.

You might find you feel quite peaceful after several minutes of deep breathing. It will help you create a state of quiet alertness where you are calm yet focused.

When you are ready, imagine you are a beautiful spiritual being of divine light. The light is centered in your chest and belly.

Continue breathing and allow your image to grow. Allow it to expand until it fills your entire body.

Next, imagine how your body will look and feel when it is an accurate physical representation of your beautiful spirit.

Take your time. There is no need to rush. Stay with your image as long as you want.

When I do this exercise, the body I imagine has no pain or sickness. It is strong and healthy, capable of almost anything. I feel wonderful, calm, and very much alive.

What did you imagine? How did it feel?

Spend some time writing or journaling about your experience. Write about how you felt and what your image looked like. Include anything that comes to you.

Repeat this exercise every day until it becomes second nature to see your Self as a spiritual being. Over time, you will embody the divine light you've imagined and physical healing will follow.

CHAPTER TWO

YOUR TRUE SELF

"You don't have a soul . . . You are a soul. You have a body, temporarily."
— WALTER M. MILLER, JR.

YOU ARE SO MUCH MORE THAN THE HUMAN BODY you inhabit. You have a body. It's the form you have taken, the house you live in while you're here on Earth. But your body isn't who or what you are.

You are a spiritual being created by the divine. What you think of as your spirit is who you are. That soul of yours is your true Self.

If you're not already doing so, change the way you think. Starting today, whenever you think of your Self, think spirit.

You were created in the image of the divine. The divine is life and love. This means that you, too, are life and love. In addition to thinking of your Self as spirit, imagine you are life and love living in a human body.

Your true Self is the inner spiritual essence that can't be seen by the human eye or touched by the human hand. You are the life force, the spiritual glue that holds the atoms, molecules, and cells together. You, quite literally, are the energy that keeps your body strong, healthy, and alive.

In other words, it's your presence that makes your body a

living organism. You are so critically important that without you, your body would die.

While you are here on earth, you and your body live and work together. You're a team. You fill your body with the life force that keeps it alive. Your body allows you to experience everything this life has to offer.

But, when all is said and done, you are separate. You will live on after your body dies. You are timeless. Eternal.

You know that voice in your head? You probably think that voice is who you are. I know I did.

I spent quite a bit of my life thinking the voice in my head was me. But I have come to an amazing and powerful realization, one that has set me free. The voice in my head isn't me. It's an imposter.

You're not the voice in your head, either. That is the voice of your ego. If you mistake that voice to be yours, you will suffer. You'll suffer because your ego is an endlessly negative judgment machine.

Your brain or thinking mind isn't you any more than any other part of your body is. Your leg is not who you are and neither is your brain.

Your brain isn't a bad thing. It's a very useful tool. But, like all tools, it can cause problems if it isn't used properly. It's great for making schedules and doing complex mathematics. But it has no idea how to love, accept without judgment, or create intimate relationships.

Fortunately, like the rest of your body, it isn't who you are. It doesn't define, or even begin to describe, the real you. The truth is, your brain will never quite be able to grasp who and what you are.

It will make up things about you that make logical sense. But your existence as a spiritual being isn't particularly logical. You, like the divine, exist beyond intellectual understanding.

The thoughts you hear as the voice in your head will generally lead you away from your Self. Even worse, it will make all sorts of negative and damaging statements about you and others. It is the source of all your negativity. Your mind is judgmental and critical, while you are loving and accepting. Your mind creates separation. You seek intimacy.

Almost every critical, judgmental thing you think about your Self comes from your mind or ego. They are almost always untrue. You'll find peace and contentment when you uncouple your sense of Self from your thoughts.

Your true Self doesn't speak a human language. Your language is love. Your words are sensations and feelings.

You can start to get reacquainted with your true Self by turning your awareness below the neck. Your inner voice, which is the voice of your true Self, speaks through the subtle sensations and feelings in your body. That's where you know something is true even if you can't explain it.

I suggest thinking of your body as your faithful and loving servant. It will serve you faithfully right up to the last moment of its life. The very best you can do is love it in return and show gratitude for all it provides. The better you treat it, the better it will treat you.

The more alive you allow your true Self to be, the more alive your body will be. This is because you are the life force your body thrives on. And a vital, healthy body is a great place to live.

Your true Self is a spiritual being. Spirituality comes first. But you must give your body what it needs. No matter how strong and centered within your Self you might be, if you don't tend to your body, it won't be healthy.

It's just that our focus as human beings has gotten skewed. We focus most of our attention on the physical world. This leads us to think that health is all about the physical.

Instead of starting with spirit and moving outward from there, when it comes to health, you're probably focused almost entirely on your body. You forget about the power of your true Self.

Unfortunately, trying to create health through physical means alone doesn't work very well. It's like trying to build a house with a weak foundation. It might work for a while, but it soon collapses.

You (the true Self) are the foundation upon which your house (body) is built. The stronger the foundation, the stronger and more durable the house will be.

When you can be your Self, your spiritual light and non-judgmental presence will transform your health and your life.

All you have to do is move your focus from the voice in your head to your inner voice, the voice of your true Self. The more you listen, the more peaceful you'll be and the healthier your body will become.

When you find your inner voice, you find the voice of your true Self. Bring that to life through the body you occupy and it will heal.

BE YOUR SELF AND BE WELL!

||||||||||||||||||||||||||||||||||||||||||||||||||||||||||||||||||||||||||||||||||||||||||||||

❧ HEALING EXERCISE

Listening to Your Body

Find a quiet, comfortable place to sit. The way you sit isn't particularly important. You can sit on a chair or on the floor. You can use some other position if it feels right for you. The goal is to be comfortable and relaxed, calm and alert.

Once you're comfortable, focus on your breathing. Breathe

slowly, rhythmically, and deeply. Some people like to breathe in through the nose and out through the mouth. If you find that appeals to you, try it. If not, don't worry; it isn't necessary.

Follow the air as it moves in and out of your body. Spend a few minutes doing nothing but sitting and breathing.

Breathe deeply; feel your chest rise and fall. Imagine you can breathe into your belly, legs, and feet. Breathe into every part of your body. As you do, notice any sensations that exist there.

After you've been breathing this way for several minutes, notice how you feel. I expect you will feel calm, peaceful, and content. That is the natural state of your true Self.

Allow your Self to be with this awareness and simply enjoy how you feel.

When you're ready, ask your Self the following questions.

Who would I be without the thoughts in my head?

If I stopped thinking, what would remain?

Allow your Self to respond. Notice the things that come to you without judging or resisting them. Simply notice how you respond.

Pay particular attention to any contrast or conflict between your thoughts and the awareness you get from your body.

Every moment you spend with the feelings and sensations of your body is a moment free from the judgments and negativity of your thoughts. That is where you find the peace of your true Self.

Spend some time writing or journaling about your experience.

Repeat this exercise often. You might make it a regular part of your daily practice.

CHAPTER THREE

YOU AND YOUR BODY

" . . . the body resembles a garment. Go, seek the one who wears it;
don't kiss a piece of cloth."

— RUMI

I MUST ADMIT, I'VE LIVED MUCH OF MY LIFE THINK-ing of my Self as the voice in my head.

This has had major consequences. The voice in my head is very judgmental. It spews an endless stream of negativity and is focused almost entirely on what's wrong: with me, with others, and with the world around me. If I am the voice in my head, I am a negative, judgmental, and unloving person.

Fortunately, I've come to realize the voice in my head is not me after all. What a relief! I would hate to be what my thoughts say I am.

What do your thoughts say about you?

I've also come to realize the human body I live in is just that: the body I live in. I am the inner spirit, not the human body you can see and touch.

It is the same for you. You are a spiritual being. Your body is the biological house where you live.

Even though you and your body are not the same, you need

each other. You are a team and must work together. Neither you nor your body could live without the other.

You can't be a human being without a human body. And your body can't be a living organism without you. Your relationship serves both of you simultaneously.

While your ego will lie and deceive, there is nothing but nonjudgmental awareness and truth contained within your body. You can access the wisdom of your body at any time. It will help you remember who you are. One of the core purposes of your body is to lead you back to your Self.

You are here on Earth to learn, grow, and experience everything life has to offer. Your body is the gift that makes this experience possible.

Your body loves you like no other. It is your closest and most loyal friend. It will serve you well and never let you down. You give it life, and it gives you every feeling and sensation you need.

Take good care of your body. Only do things you and your body both love and enjoy. Abandon or minimize the time you spend doing things that are detrimental for either of you.

Above all else, be your Self. Always remember that your true Self is a spiritual being. Tend to you and your needs first, and then turn to the needs of your body.

Be patient with your Self. This is a process that might take a while. If you're like me, you haven't been thinking of your Self as a spiritual being for very long. But if you stick with it, it will eventually become second nature.

Think, speak, and act spirit. Take a risk and be who and what you are every moment of every day. When you do, your body will change and heal.

Creating health and well-being isn't complicated. It's easy. I'll give you a simple formula for creating optimal health and well-being.

Focus most of your time and energy on the fulfillment of your soul. Live freely and passionately as your true Self.

Then, love and nourish your body. Eat only the best food. No junk. Exercise regularly and make it fun. Laugh often, especially with those you love. Breathe deeply and drink water throughout the day. Sleep so that you feel rested and alert when you wake up.

Consider this liberating concept. Your body doesn't do anything *to* you. It only does things *for* you. You may not always like what your body provides, but you can rest assured that it is for you. Serving you and teaching you are its only purposes. You may not initially understand what it attempts to teach you. But if you can embrace the sensations you get from your body as messages that it provides to help you, you will eventually come to understand why they are there.

Listen to your body. Pay attention and you will learn. As you learn, the sensations will change. Any pain will diminish or completely go away. Sickness will resolve. Once the lesson is learned, the teacher is no longer necessary.

Because of my profession, people usually come to see me when they're in pain. They want me to make it go away. But even if I could make the pain stop, I might not be helping because there is always a reason for the pain. There is some lesson to be learned, some wisdom to be gained. My job is to help you get to the bottom of it and discover what the pain is saying. Once you do, the pain will stop.

If I listen carefully and ask the right questions, you will almost always tell me what is happening below the surface.

Physical pain is often an indication of something deeper and more meaningful. It's simply the voice of some other dysfunction. Pain is the way your body gets your attention. When you're in pain, your body is trying to tell you something. And it's likely something about you.

The real problem almost always comes from your inability to be who you are, feel what you need to feel, or say what you need to say.

Bonnie's story illustrates this concept perfectly. It's a very common pattern, one I've seen again and again. Bonnie came in because her back hurt. She hadn't been injured. It just started hurting one day and hadn't stopped no matter what she did. It gradually got to the point where it was affecting her sleep and ability to work.

Her husband's work was unsteady and his income fluctuated, sometimes dramatically. The financial uncertainty made her anxious. She never knew whether they'd have enough money or not. As a result, Bonnie worked hard at jobs she didn't like. She felt like she had to work hard to provide her family some measure of financial stability.

I listened. I asked a few questions. It all spilled out.

It suddenly hit her. Bonnie realized she was symbolically carrying the weight of her entire family on her back. The back pain was her body's way of helping her discover the truth.

Bonnie's husband loved his work even though his income varied. She didn't want to hurt his feelings, so she bit her tongue and did her best to keep it together. But she couldn't bottle it up any longer. Her back pain was the wake-up call she needed.

She cried as she let it out. I watched her breathing slow down and get deeper. Her shoulders dropped and she relaxed into her chair. Her entire posture changed within minutes.

By the time she finished telling her story, her back pain was almost gone.

Her body had done her a great service. The pain was a powerful messenger for a deeper issue. Once she got the message, she no longer needed the pain.

It doesn't matter whether you're sick or in pain. You might even be depressed or facing challenging relationships. No matter what is happening, the first and most powerful tool is bringing your Self back to full presence.

Nothing has the power to heal like you do. When you bring your Self back to full engagement with life, you might not need any other remedy. Your power to heal might be all that's needed.

Think of it like this: Your job is to say yes to life. Say yes even when you don't like it and when it hurts. Say yes to everything life lays at your doorstep. You will never be given more than you can handle.

Above all else, remember that you and your body are not the same. Your body is physical. You are spiritual. Your body can get sick but you cannot. You can experience pain, but you are never in pain.

Reinforce the strength of your awareness that you are a spiritual being of immense power. Live it. Breathe it. Speak and act it. You and your body will both grow stronger and healthier.

BE YOUR SELF AND BE WELL!

||||||||||||||||||||||||||||||||||||||||||||||||||||||||||||||||||||||||||||||||||||||

❧ HEALING EXERCISE

Be Real When Someone Asks How You Are

People ask me how I am all the time. It's become the standard greeting in my part of the world.

"How are you?"

"Fine. How are you?"

"Not bad."

We might as well just say, "Hello."

Join me in starting a little cultural revolution. Let's bring meaning and substance back into our greetings. Here's how.

When people ask me how I am, I stop for a moment to let my inner Self respond. It's sort of like, "Hmm, great question! How am I? I'll check."

No matter what is happening on the surface, I pause and turn my awareness inward. I let my true Self respond. When I do, I reconnect with who and how I am. And the wonderful thing is, I am always something really great.

I smile and answer, "Thanks for asking. I'm super awesome!"

I have never stopped to listen to my true Self and heard anything negative. It's always something good, something positive.

I share the truth of how I am. It is a wonderfully positive affirmation of the essential me. I feel even better as a result. And it gives the other person an opportunity to respond in kind. Everyone is uplifted.

Try it for your Self and see what happens. Instead of giving the automatic "fine," pause briefly and check in with your inner Self. Be real about how you are on the inside. It's fun. You'll strengthen your own spiritual presence. You'll break the monotony and give people a chance to share something of substance.

Instead of empty words, you can share something significant about your Self. And when you share your inner truth, you open the door to greater intimacy.

After you've worked with this greeting exercise for a while, do some writing or journaling about your experiences. Include how you felt and how others responded to you.

CHAPTER FOUR

YOU ARE WHOLE

"Joy is a return to the deep harmony of body, mind, and spirit
that was yours at birth and that can be yours again.
That openness to love, that capacity for wholeness
with the world around you, is still within you."
— DEEPAK CHOPRA

YOU'RE NOT DAMAGED OR BROKEN; YOU'RE WHOLE.

It doesn't matter what might have happened during your life, it didn't change you on the inside where it matters most.

Divorce, bankruptcy, addictions, and abusive relationships are all too common. And they are only a few of the many challenging situations we may find ourselves engaged in.

I'm sure you've experienced trials in your life. Maybe you've lived through terrible things. Without minimizing what you've gone through, I would like you to start to uncouple your sense of Self from what has happened.

You are a creation of love. You were made by love, as love, and for love. This is the bottom line. This is the awareness that makes healing possible. It doesn't matter what may or may not have happened—you are a whole, loving, spiritual being. That never changes.

You are a creation of the divine, made in the image of the divine. Nothing in this world can alter that. Make that your new inner story.

The thing we humans do, and we are supremely good at it, is make up stories. Then we start to believe the stories we make up and our suffering begins.

The stories start honestly. You want to make sense of what happened so you can find understanding. So instead of living through the experience and leaving it at that, you start to give it meaning. This is how the damage occurs.

For example, your marriage ends in divorce. You decide it was your fault. You didn't do enough or try hard enough. You weren't perfect and made mistakes. You couldn't change the other person or make them love you. You must be flawed. It proves you're an unlovable failure. You're broken and must suffer.

Everyone does their own version of this process. No one is immune. We make up the stories that cause our suffering.

The story will always say you were wounded, damaged, or broken. You are the reason the terrible things happened. You will never be whole again. You will never be able to trust again. You will never know love again. It goes on and on.

Once you've created your story, you will live in fear that it will happen again. The world becomes a fearful place, full of the potential for more pain.

Your fears will cause you to try and control your Self and the world around you. Careful, vigilant control is the only way you will feel safe. And careful, vigilant control is not living.

To heal, you must return to the experience. You must allow every response you had to express itself in its entirety. This is the hard work of healing. Healing takes place when you can separate your sense of Self from the things that have happened. Healing is shining the light of spiritual truth on your stories and beginning to see that they are not true. They were the source of your suffering, not the things that happened.

Your pain is part of the energy that lives on inside you after the event has happened. You can be you or you can be the pain. You can't be both.

To regain your freedom and to live without fear, all the energy associated with the pain must be expressed. If you can let it out, you will regain the freedom to be you, whole and complete.

If you hold it in, life will poke it. It will leak out. No matter how well you control your Self and your environment, you will end up living out the trauma again and again.

The beliefs that dictate who you can be and what you can do in life come from the stories you make up about your experiences. They are almost all negative and Self-limiting.

The beliefs that accompany your stories will reinforce the perception that you are flawed. Above all, they will stop you from being the whole, loving being you are.

To see the truth of your inner wholeness, you must look through the human body as if it doesn't exist. You must look for the whole spiritual being that lives inside the human body. To see it you have to look with your inner awareness. Reach out with the hands of perception that extend from your heart and soul. You can't see it with your human eyes, but you can feel it with your presence. Feel it and you will know it.

Our differences are skin-deep; they are no different than clothes. You can change your clothing all you want. No matter what you put on, you're still the same person. What you see on the outside is not who you are.

Race and nationality, age and gender, have and have-not, none of these truly matter. Nothing is real but unity and oneness. As spiritual beings, all are one, whole and complete. This truth includes you.

Healing allows you to love everything about your Self. It allows you to recognize others as family. You're not enemies. You're brothers and sisters. You're not broken. You're the image of loving wholeness.

When you heal and live as your true Self, you live as love. You bring your loving essence into the world and it touches others.

Love creates the space where everyone can heal. Love is the vehicle that carries you back to your inner awareness of wholeness. Once you see your Self as whole and undamaged, you will begin to create that image in your life.

But your stories will stand in the way unless you explore them. The story will say that you are damaged. You are not love. You are a big problem, broken and unlovable. You'll put up walls and close your Self off. You turn inward and become unreachable.

Love can no longer get through your defenses. You turn away from love and who you are at the very same time.

Suffering begins when you turn away from your essential nature as a whole, loving being. You can be whole or you can suffer. You can't do both.

This pattern of retreat, weakness, and suffering will happen over and over again. In each instance, you become a little less alive. Your pain and suffering grow as you get smaller.

It is not until you return to the pain and express it that you will be able to recover the part you lost when you made up a story and tried to control your life. You can only break the cycle by taking a risk and reopening to life even when everything indicates that you will be hurt once again.

This is part of what can make healing such a challenge. It is your fear of getting hurt that started things in the first place.

In this moment, you must look for the dim flicker of a distant light. It is there, even if you haven't been able to see it. In the face of overwhelming evidence that indicates otherwise, you must cling to the belief that you are whole and loving. You must tie a rope to that anchor and plunge into the dark waters of your pain, barely believing you'll emerge again.

Once the light returns, you will discover what you could not see before. Your experiences say absolutely nothing about you. They didn't change you. You are not damaged. You are still the whole, loving creation of the divine you have always been.

Healing can follow many different paths, yet they all end at the same place. The destination of all healing paths is the wholeness of the true Self as created by the divine.

You are a creation of the divine, whole and complete. Nothing can change that.

BE YOUR SELF AND BE WELL!

HEALING EXERCISE

See Your Self and Others as Whole

I borrowed this exercise from the author and teacher, Marianne Williamson, but I've made some changes.

Every time you look in a mirror, look yourself in the eye and say, "I am whole and loving."

As you go about your day, look everyone you meet in the eye and say to your Self, "You and I are whole, loving beings."

Notice how you respond to doing this exercise. Make note of any thoughts or beliefs that are triggered by it.

Pay attention to how you feel. Notice how you respond to others and how they respond to you. You might make it a regular part of the way you live your life.

Do some writing or journaling about your experiences.

CHAPTER FIVE

YOU MAKE HEALING HAPPEN

"We are not our bodies, our possessions, or our careers.
Who we are is divine love and that is infinite."
— DR. WAYNE DYER

I WANT YOU TO CHANGE THE WAY YOU THINK about health and healing. I want you to think of your Self as the power that makes healing possible.

If you're like most people, you've thought about health and healing in regards to your body. You might consider diet and exercise, maybe medicine. But there's a very good chance you haven't made the link between healing and spirituality. It's time to change that.

More than anything, you are a spiritual being. Your spirit is the power that makes healing possible. At its roots, healing is a spiritual pursuit.

Very little healing comes from what you do. The real power to heal comes from who you are.

Your physical ailments get your attention. And they, in turn, get you focused on your body and its needs.

But physical ailments are almost always superficial manifestations of the real trouble. The real problem is that you have limited your true Self. Focus your efforts on recovering your sense of Self instead of just trying to stop your physical ailments with physical interventions. You will be far more successful and everything will happen with more ease.

Your body will follow your lead. If you limit your Self, you limit your body. Your body will suffer and end up sick or in pain. Without the strength of your spirit, your body cannot be healthy.

You can see the power of this phenomenon in people who have given up on life. It happens frequently to the elderly who lose a spouse. Within months, they're dead too. They give up and no medicine can change that or save them.

The good news is that you are a spiritual being of immense power. You have the ability to overcome any physical illness.

When you are passionately alive, your body will have all the energy it needs to be strong and healthy. No sickness is more powerful than you.

Many people seek their purpose in life. They want to know their higher calling, to feel connected to something larger.

Maybe you are one of those people. Have you wondered why you are here and what you're meant to do?

If you distill the reason you're here down to its essence, it is quite simple and uncomplicated. You are here to be you.

The creator made you to be you. Being you is why you are here. You can think of it as your "soul purpose" in life. There is nothing more important or valuable than living as who you were created to be.

When you live as your true Self, you will feel deeply peaceful and content. And the energy of peace and contentment is among the most powerful tools for creating health and well-being.

The opposite is also true. Living as something other than who and what you are creates immense stress. The energy of stress creates all sorts of pain and sickness. Everything goes bad when you're not spiritually present. It really is the power of your spiritual presence that makes health and healing possible.

I've been working with a young woman I'll call Barbara. Like so many people, she has judged herself very harshly. She believes she is essentially unlovable and because of that, unworthy of anything good.

There are times she won't allow her Self to eat. She feels food and nourishment are too good for her.

Our treatments or interventions could be focused on food and eating, but eating is a symptom, not the problem itself. The problem is that she doesn't love her Self enough to eat well. Our therapeutic approach needs to be oriented around helping her recover her sense of Self-love.

Another thing Barbara does is isolate. She doesn't feel safe when she goes out because her Self-judgments make her sacrifice her Self. She will do just about anything anyone else wants her to do.

Her sense of value only comes from what she can do for someone else. Others' needs are far more important than anything she wants or needs. She always comes last, a slave to others. But things are changing.

Barbara has started to reconnect with her inner Self. As a result, there are times when she knows, deep down, that she is love and has value simply by being her Self. When she connects with the love inside her Self, she acts differently. She treats her Self with love and respect.

From the space of Self-love, Barbara can say no to others and yes to her Self. She doesn't isolate her Self in fear of being used. Barbara feels happy and excited to be alive. She even eats well.

Barbara has started to access the power of her loving spirit, and it is fueling her healing.

We have a lot of serious problems in the world today. They affect every aspect of life. It's a long and disturbing list. War and terrorism, environmental pollution, poverty and homelessness, and racial and religious oppression are everywhere.

Here in the US, about 25 percent of the adult population suffers from depression or anxiety. We live in fear, afraid to open our doors, even to our neighbors.

It looks like we have a multitude of unrelated problems. But the truth is, we only have one. And that problem creates all the others: we have turned away from who we are and the creator who made us.

The solution: reconnect with who we are and where we came from. Healing is the first step in solving every problem we have.

You already know just what to do. You were born with the wisdom of the divine alive inside of you. Healing is turning inward and contacting that wisdom. Solutions to every problem you have will start to appear.

Your spirit is the power that makes healing possible and provides the solutions for all problems, personal and global.

One of our greatest challenges is that we think nonstop. We live with an endless stream of negative and judgmental thoughts flowing through our minds, one negative thing after another.

Make a point of listening to your thoughts. Be an observer. Listen to the voice in your head like you might listen to the radio.

Pay attention to what you hear. Notice how much of it is negative and judgmental. Pay attention to the things you know aren't true.

Believing the voice in your head is what leads to most of your problems. To find peace, you must turn away from your thoughts. You must reconnect with the peace of your true Self, the Self that exists below the neck.

There are many tools you can use to focus your awareness

on your Self instead of your thoughts. There are too many to list, but some include meditation, yoga, exercise, prayer, and quiet time in nature.

They all have one thing in common. They help you stay present and contact the power of your spirit. Choose the one(s) that work for you and practice as often as possible.

This brings me to another of my clients.

Susan's doctor had given her a serious diagnosis that scared her. To treat it, he recommended drugs that had serious side effects. It stopped her in her tracks. She came to see me for a second opinion, hoping there might be a less aggressive treatment without the terrible side effects.

As it worked out, the energetic, spiritual healing approach worked wonderfully for her. As Susan moved closer to her true Self, her body began to change. She lost weight. Her energy improved. She literally started looking younger and feeling healthier. Her pain decreased significantly and became occasional instead of constant.

People noticed and started asking what she was doing, all wanting to know what diet she was following or if she had started a new workout. Some even asked if she'd had cosmetic surgery.

We see the physical body. But we're the inside, not the outside. It's precisely when our inner beauty shines through that we look the most alive and beautiful.

Without realizing it, people were witnessing her inner change. They couldn't put their finger on it, but they could tell something significant had changed.

It was the outward manifestation of her inner beauty that was transforming her. People saw her spirit shine through. It was changing her body.

Susan's healing was spiritual, not physical. The physical

changes were made possible by the power of her inner spirit. She started telling people she had healed by recovering from her former spiritual apathy.

You can do the same. You have the power to heal. All you need to do is get reconnected with the unlimited power of your spirit.

As Dr. Edward Bach, the originator of Bach Flower Remedies, said, "Disease is solely and purely corrective; it is neither vindictive nor cruel, but it is the means adopted by our own souls to point out to us our faults, to prevent our making greater errors, to hinder us from doing more harm, and to bring us back to the path of Truth and Light from which we should never have strayed."

When pain and sickness appear, it is time to stop and listen. Your body is trying to tell you something very important. It's trying to tell you that you have strayed from your Self. You have strayed from the spiritual path you're meant to walk.

The symptoms you experience through the vehicle of your body are not being done to you—they are created for you. They are not a form of punishment. They are the very essence of love. Every symptom you have is an expression of love sent to you from your body to help you recover your true Self.

When you reconnect with your true Self, you access the power of your spirit, and physical healing will take place.

As a spiritual being, you are the life force that organizes and animates your body. Your body responds to you. Being passionately alive creates the energy for physical health.

Miracles can happen. They happen when you reconnect with your spiritual essence and live as who you were created to be.

BE YOUR SELF AND BE WELL!

❧ HEALING EXERCISE

Make Spirituality a Part of Your Daily Life

Choose one thing you can do every day that will help focus your attention on who you are as a spiritual being. It could be a prayer or a meditation. Affirmations and quotes from spiritual teachers are powerful reminders. It could even be as simple as a long walk in nature.

It doesn't matter what you choose. What matters is choosing something that helps you focus on who you are on the inside instead of what you think. It's also important to choose something you enjoy doing and something you will do every day.

Make a commitment to incorporate your activity of spiritual awareness into your daily life. You are making a commitment to be your Self and heal.

Put it in your schedule. Make it a nonnegotiable.

Once you've incorporated spirit into your daily life, write or journal about your experience. Include anything you have learned and any ways in which your life has changed.

CHAPTER SIX

HEALING AND CURE

"The physician should not treat the disease but the patient who is suffering from it."
— MAIMONIDES

HEALING AND CURE ARE TWO DIFFERENT THINGS. Like you and your body, they are related. This contributes to the confusion and reinforces the perception that they're the same. They're close, like twins. But like twins, while they might look the same, they're not.

You can heal without achieving cure. And sometimes you can cure sickness without healing.

It makes more sense when you recall that you and your body are not the same.

Healing is for you, the true Self that is spiritual. Cure is for your human body. Healing and cure are separate just like you and your body are separate.

Modern medicine largely ignores your spirit. It's the elephant in the room that nobody talks about. You, as a spiritual being, are ignored. It's almost as if the medicine matters more than you.

The truth is, you are what is most important. It's not your body, the disease, or the medicine: it's you.

To be truly successful and lasting, healing therapies must include you. Without the energy or life force of your spirit, your body won't be able to heal. But with you, almost anything is possible. You have unlimited healing power.

What I have seen is that any cure achieved without healing will be temporary at best. Without healing and accessing the strength of your spiritual presence, all you'll be able to achieve is rebandaging a wound that won't heal. In many cases, it simply won't matter what cure you try to create. It won't work. No medicine can make up for your lack of spiritual presence.

The undeniable truth is that your body can't do it on its own. It needs you. Without you, your body is little more than an empty shell. If you aren't present, your body won't be able to create or maintain health and well-being.

Unfortunately, even though your spirit is immensely powerful, healing doesn't always create a cure.

It's taken me a long time to accept this. It has troubled me. It seemed to me that if healing was so powerful, it should always create a cure. But the truth is, it doesn't.

You can heal, be spiritually present, and not cure your pain and sickness.

It's best to pursue healing because it helps you feel alive and connected to the divine. If you pursue healing only because it might cure your disease, there's a good chance you will end up disappointed.

I am very grateful to have access to the wonders of modern medicine. Today's doctors do amazing things. Using the power of modern medicine, you can sometimes cure your disease without giving the slightest thought to your spirit. This allows you to be complacent and ignore who you are. And it leads to deeper problems. You live disconnected from your source, alive but not really living.

For many people, the idea that healing is a spiritual pursuit is new and revolutionary. This is exactly how I used to feel. I never stopped to think it through. But now that I have, it makes perfect sense to me.

It cannot be any other way. If I am a spiritual being, I am a key component in any healing or cure.

Healing isn't outside in. It's inside out.

Far and away, the best results come when we can work with body and spirit together. This creates real holistic care—care that has the power to heal and cure at the same time.

When you are passionately alive in a body that is loved and cared for, health and well-being are almost certain. Working with both as one is the way to create changes that are hard to imagine, changes that are almost miraculous.

Margaret's story is a great example.

She originally came in after receiving a Crohn's disease diagnosis. Her doctor had recommended a powerful drug that would help control her symptoms.

Her doctor also told her that her condition probably couldn't be cured. The best they could do was manage the situation, try to keep it from getting worse, and help her live with it.

Margaret went home and googled the condition and the drug her doctor had prescribed. She was shocked to learn that most people who take the medication never get off it. Plus it had serious side effects. She said to her Self, "There's got to be a better way."

She asked people if they knew someone they could recommend. One person she asked happened to be my client. Margaret called and made an appointment. She came in not knowing what to expect. She hadn't tried alternative or holistic medicine before. But she knew she didn't want to take the drug, so she was willing to try something new.

I did an energetic hands-on healing during our first session. I also recommended dietary changes and nutritional supplements.

Margaret took what I had to offer and ran with it. She did everything I asked.

Fast-forward a few years.

I recently saw Margaret following a checkup with her current medical doctor. By all medical measurements, Margaret is doing great. There are no indications of the disease that first brought her in, a disease she was told couldn't be cured.

Margaret has been able to heal and cure her sickness without drugs or surgery. Her primary tool was her own spiritual awakening. As she reconnected with her true Self, it facilitated other changes in her life. Those changes helped create even more change and deepened her spiritual connection. She cleaned up her diet and started a daily practice of morning prayer and meditation. Barbara started reading books on spirituality and mindfulness. Instead of going to an occasional yoga class, she now goes regularly.

This is the power of spiritual presence. Access it and you can heal. Once you heal, almost any cure is possible.

At times, drugs and surgery are necessary. But they force your body to change, and the results always come at a cost. Every drug has side effects. Outside of joy and deep contentment, there are no side effects associated with spiritual awakening.

Some of the most profound experiences of healing are facilitated by serious illness.

Healing may not change the course of the illness at all. For many people, the most intense healing takes place as their bodies are dying. As they face the end, their eyes are opened. They come to see what truly matters in life.

The death of your body brings with it an opportunity for

deep and powerful healing. Death isn't a failure, it's an integral part of the human experience.

Bronnie Ware, a nurse who counseled people who were dying, took the time to listen and record their regrets. The top five regrets of the dying are powerful and insightful.

"I wish I'd had the courage to live a life true to my Self."

"I wish I hadn't worked so hard."

"I wish I'd had the courage to express my feelings."

"I wish I had stayed in touch with my friends."

"I wish I had let my Self be happier."

We can use these statements as models for life. Be true to your Self. Take time to enjoy the day. Express your feelings. Stay in touch with those you love. And, above all, be happy.

Make a commitment to your Self. No one else will do it for you. Live each day so that you have no regrets at the end of your life.

You will be free when the strength of your belief in your identity as a spiritual being is unshakable. It won't matter nearly as much if death comes for you today, tomorrow, or next year. Today is as good a day as any to die.

The only thing that endures is you. Healing is placing your awareness on the power of your eternal spirit and letting that dictate your life decisions.

You might choose to start each day with this simple affirmation:

Today I will love and care for my body. I will live passionately as the spiritual being I am. And I will enjoy whatever this day brings, knowing it is a gift from the divine.

Cure will cease to hold its critical importance once you know who you are. You will begin to understand that it doesn't matter nearly as much as you once thought. If you need sickness, you will receive it. If you need cure, you will receive that too. You will be able to relax, knowing that everything is guided by the divine.

With divine guidance, miracles can and will happen. Your spiritual presence has the power to change anything and everything.

You can start expecting miraculous cures and know they're absolutely normal. Together, we can create a new world where healing and the miraculous cures that follow are the expected norm.

BE YOUR SELF AND BE WELL!

〰 HEALING EXERCISE

Imagine the Death of Your Body

Find a quiet, comfortable place to sit and breathe deeply.

Breathe slowly and rhythmically, following the air as it moves in and out of your body. Feel your chest rise and fall. Feel your abdomen expand and contract. Breathe for a few minutes; allow your Self to become calm and centered.

Once you feel calm, present, and relaxed, ask your Self the following question.

"What would I do if I knew my body was going to die today?"

Instead of listening to your thoughts about death, listen to how the real you responds. Listen to the awareness of your true Self that comes from the sensations in your chest and belly. It will be a simple knowing or awareness.

What would you do? Would you do anything?

Notice how you feel. Do you feel scared? Do you feel calm and accepting? Are you at peace?

Make a commitment to live for today, right now. There is no tomorrow. And your ability to live passionately in the moment is the fuel that creates health and healing.

Spend some time writing or journaling about your experience.

CHAPTER SEVEN

LISTEN TO YOUR PAIN

"The cure for pain is in the pain."
— RUMI

PAIN IS A GREAT MOTIVATOR. IT INSPIRES US TO act like nothing else. Unfortunately, we treat pain as the enemy. We fight it and resist it. We take drugs to make it go away. But we might be cheating ourselves.

If you're like most people, you clench your muscles and hold your breath when you experience pain. You'll do almost anything you can to make it stop.

The more you resist pain, the stronger it gets. Trying to push it away causes it to push back, giving it strength and intensity.

As the best-selling author and spiritual teacher Eckhart Tolle says, "Whatever you fight, you strengthen, and what you resist, persists."

Instead of fighting and resisting, a better approach is to make friends with your pain. Open your arms and move closer, so close you become one. If you can do that, it will tell you why it's there. Pain is a messenger. If you can develop a relationship and listen, it will teach you.

As I work with my clients, I always tell them to breathe into their pain. This shifts their focus from resistance to acceptance. As they breathe into their pain, it almost always gets less intense.

When you stop resisting your pain, it won't hurt as much. And you'll discover things you didn't know before. I suggest you stop thinking of the sensation as pain. Explore it like something you've never encountered before. Instead of calling it pain, use other words to describe it.

Is it hot or cold? Is it pressure? Is it burning or tingling? How would you describe it if you couldn't use the word pain?

Let go of your prior judgments, move closer, and get to know it. It won't be as threatening and you'll be able to relax. As you relax, you'll feel better. Nothing hurts as much when you're calm, accepting, and relaxed.

Fighting pain doesn't get you what you want. When you're fighting, you're not peaceful. And, if you're like most people, inner peace is something you want more than just about anything else.

Lack of peace causes suffering and makes life more difficult in just about every way.

The hidden truth is that loss of peace creates most pain. You might say you'll be peaceful once the pain is gone. But it's not the pain that stops you from being peaceful, it's you.

You might not believe me until you have experienced it, but I'll share a little secret with you: you can feel pain and be peaceful at the same time. All you have to do is turn your awareness from the pain in your body to the peace of your true Self.

Your body might be sending you pain messages, but you're not in pain. There is no pain in the realm of spirit.

The people I work with usually come in because they have pain. But more often than not, their pain is the top layer, the tip of the iceberg. The pain hints at what lies beneath. To help them, I must find out what the pain represents.

The pain is just the starting point. It's rarely the problem. The real problem is something deeper, something about who they are and the way they live.

Over time, I have come to appreciate that whatever might be hidden under the pain is what has stopped them from being at peace—with themselves, with others, and with life.

If we can get down to the root of whatever has taken over and displaced their awareness of inner peace, the healing will begin. Within the pain are the answers we're looking for.

Pain distracts you from your Self. You lose touch with the peace of your Self and move into stress. Stress increases pain and initiates more disease.

Peace and stress are polar opposites. You can be your Self and feel peaceful. Or you can focus on things that aren't you and suffer the damaging effects of stress.

This is a problem that medicine cannot fix. No medicine can get you reconnected with your true Self. It's something you have to do for your Self.

Yoga and meditation are powerful tools for getting reconnected with your Self. Exercise and walks in nature work well. The deep breathing I recommend for the healing exercises is powerful precisely because it helps you reconnect with your Self.

The magic isn't in the technique, it's in you. Use any tool you like. If it helps you get reconnected with the peace of your true Self, it will help you move out of pain and heal.

Peace cannot be taken away from you because peace is who and what you are. This is the way the creator made you. Nothing can change that. Turn your awareness away from the sensation of pain and back to your true Self. You will, once again, be peaceful.

Even when every outside form of evidence would indicate otherwise, it is not the external world that is exerting its influence on you. You are responding to the world and exerting a force upon your Self. You are a spiritual being. Only you and the divine have the power to touch you.

Every painful situation, whether it's physical pain or emotional pain, exists to teach you something. It's a messenger speaking directly to you and for you.

As the author Eckhart Tolle has said, "Whenever anything negative happens to you, there is a deep lesson concealed within it."

Peace comes with accepting whatever challenges life brings, knowing it is happening for your benefit. It isn't being done to you. It's not a punishment. It's a loving gift from the creator, meant to help you learn and return to your Self.

Pain is a messenger. Peace is who and what you are. Pain is always an indication that you have lost touch with your Self.

Stop resisting. Explore your pain and it will lead you back to your Self and the peace you are.

BE YOUR SELF AND BE WELL!

||||||||||||||||||||||||||||||||||||||||||||||||||||||||||||||||||||||||||||||||||||||

❧ HEALING EXERCISE

Listen to Your Pain

Find a quiet, comfortable place to sit and breathe deeply.

Breathe slowly, deeply, and rhythmically. Breathe until you're calm, centered, and relaxed. Allow your Self to be carried away by your breath until it is your entire world.

If there is a part of your body that is giving you messages of pain, turn your awareness to it.

Seek only to get to know the sensation. Explore it with open curiosity. Forget prior experiences and allow your Self to explore it like it is something you've never encountered before. Let the sensations speak to you.

Try to find words to describe the sensation without using the word "pain." How does it feel?

When you're ready, ask, "Why do I have this pain? What is it trying to tell me? Am I the pain, or am I peace?"

Allow your Self to discover the answers.

Repeat this exercise daily for as long as you need to receive the message and understand the deeper meaning behind the pain. Take action on anything you've discovered.

Finally, do some writing or journaling about your experience.

CHAPTER EIGHT

YOU ARE LOVE

*"Your task is not to seek for love, but merely to seek and find all
the barriers within yourself that you have built against it."*

— RUMI

LOVE. IT'S WEIRD AND POWERFUL, OFTEN CON-fusing. But what is it?

Is love an action or activity?

People talk about giving and receiving love or even making love. What is it you give, receive, or make?

Take a moment to think about it and explore your beliefs about love. See if you can come up with a clear, simple answer.

Love is really very simple. It's a feeling coupled with awareness.

Love is the sensation you feel when you are aware of who you are, your true Self. When you contact your Self, you feel love. Stated another way, you are the love you feel.

Love is also your response to getting in touch with the true Self of another.

When you experience another's spiritual presence, you will feel love. It is your response to feeling who that person really is as a spiritual being. Love is how you react to another's spiritual presence.

You can't be present and experience the spiritual presence of another person without feeling love.

There is only one true love. All others are cheap imposters. Real love is the sensation that comes from knowing your true Self, the true Self of another, or the divine. Any sensation created by any other experience is not love.

Because love is a feeling, it can't be given or taken away. It can only be felt. The feeling of love will provoke many sensations in your body. But they exist solely and completely inside of you. Unless you tell them, no other people know what you're feeling.

You can feel the power of love but you cannot give it to others or make them feel it.

When you feel love, part of what you feel is the response of your body to the energy of spiritual presence. Your body responds to love more powerfully than any other energy.

The feeling you call love is your body responding to you or your palpable awareness of another's spiritual essence.

That contact makes your spirit sing. Your inner energetic vibration rises and intensifies. Your body responds and you feel the incredible awakening of your body and spirit and say, "I'm in love!"

Love is who and what you are. Your spiritual essence is the love you feel. It is what the divine created when he created you.

We human beings regularly act as if we can make other people love us. If we just do and say the right things, others will love us.

Similarly, we cling to the belief that love is earned. It's your actions that make you either lovable or unlovable. Do the right things and you're lovable. Do the wrong things and you're unlovable.

The human notion of being unlovable is complete fantasy. You were created by love, as love, and for love. Love is not earned. Love cannot be given or taken away. Love is who and what you are.

Beyond your name and the roles you play—more profound than anything you can see and touch—love identifies the real you. You might think of it as your middle name or the name you had before your parents gave you the one you use today. It is the way you began life.

You can't make another person love you. The way others respond is entirely up to them. You have little to no control over it.

Several years ago, I registered to attend a retreat called "Healers Evolving." I didn't know much about it, but the name spoke to me.

I thought of my Self as a healer and what that meant to me. It excited me as I imagined what might happen at a retreat where healers were evolving. There isn't much that gets me going like the prospect of inner growth and spiritual awakening.

I went expecting a week of deep inner work and healing. It was a long drive, so I used the time to listen to books on tape. I listened to the medical intuitive Caroline Myss and the spiritual teacher Marianne Williamson. I listened to the profound words of author Oriah Mountain Dreamer. Using their words of wisdom as fuel, I moved deeper into my Self.

The retreat was held on a remote island. So, we had to take a boat to get there.

It was lovely. I sat quietly enjoying the warm sun and cool breeze on my face. The sunlight reflected off the water, sparkling on the waves created by the boat. I said little, simply enjoying the experience.

A couple days later, the contact person and organizer of the retreat asked to speak with me. "Were you stoned when you arrived at the landing?" I was shocked. For a moment, I simply stared at her. I finally managed to say, "Wow, uh no."

Her interpretation of my blissful state of presence was that I was stoned. But I was anything but stoned. I was high on spiritual presence.

Spiritual awakening requires quiet awareness and inner focus. I arrived at the landing already deeply engaged in my own inner process. My intention was to continue my own inner awakening, to truly be a healer evolving.

I enjoyed the boat ride in silence. I was focused on my Self and the life exploding all around me. I didn't speak about what I was doing and feeling. If someone had asked, I would have been happy to share what I was experiencing. But no one asked.

We are so unaccustomed to quiet presence that we often don't know what to make of it. This person's interpretation was that I was stoned, and it was completely wrong.

I felt disappointed at first. But I made the most of it. I believe that the hand of the divine is present in all things and everything happens for a reason. I got to spend a week on a beautiful, remote island with abundant time to be quiet, pray, and connect with my true Self. It was a spiritually fulfilling adventure.

You never know how others are going to respond to you. They will think what they're going to think. They will feel what they're going to feel. You have very little to do with it.

In the words of the singer-songwriter Paul Simon, "A man hears what he wants to hear and disregards the rest."

Unless you are very present and thereby able to be an open, neutral observer, most of what you experience is your own little fantasy world. This is especially true when it comes to love.

You may believe you are responsible for making another feel loved. If you do the right things and say the right things, those around you will know you love them.

Unfortunately, as illustrated by my story, you have almost no control or influence over how others respond. They'll feel love if they're open to it. If not, they won't. The best you can do is just to stop trying and be your Self.

If you find your Self trying to make others feel loved, stop and ask your Self why. Why is it so important to you that they feel loved? What will it do for you? Not them, you?

The inner truth to discover is that your actions are for you. They come from the belief that if they feel loved it will do something for you. What you're doing is trying to give another what you want your Self.

When you work hard to make others feel loved, you are almost always trying to make up for your own inner love deficiency. Because of this, your actions are not expressions of love. They are requests for love masquerading as expressions of love.

You'll never find love outside of your Self. It doesn't exist out there. You must find it in your Self before you can experience it anywhere else.

Feeling love can motivate your actions. Feeling love can inspire your words and deeds. But love and actions are separate and distinct.

Love is infinitely more than saying "I love you." Love is more than giving someone a gift, no matter how generous the gift might be. Love is more than caring for the sick. Love is more than a phone call on Mother's Day.

No words or actions can adequately convey the essence of love. Love is the divine energy that underlies and motivates the giving. True love is allowing the love you are to respond to the love in another in any way it takes form.

Sometimes the words and actions of others feel hurtful and unloving when they are truly expressions of love. This happens when their actions bring to light the areas where you are not being your true Self. Their actions push your buttons and provoke your inner pain.

For example, you are drinking too much. Your friend calls you on it. But instead of owning the fact that you have been drinking too much, you respond with an angry insult. It's not that you don't know you've been drinking too much—you do. It's just that if you acknowledge the drinking, you're going to have to own up to the reasons why. And that is where the real pain lies.

Calling you on your drinking is an expression of love. But in that moment, it doesn't feel like love. It feels like an attack. So, you put up your defenses and lash out to avoid the pain that started the problem in the first place.

If someone pushes your buttons and provokes your inner pain, you'll probably want to get mad and attack. That way you don't have to confront your pain.

It's way easier to lash out at another than admit to your own wounds. Instead of opening to your inner pain and the vulnerability that accompanies it, you put up a fight. You point the finger and say, "It's not me, it's them!" You try to make them the problem when they simply exposed your wounds.

When it happens, notice your reaction, but don't allow it to take over. Stop and remember the truth. They are asking you to move through your pain and come back to the love you are. Your inner pain and the story that creates it is a doorway to healing.

There is almost always deep inner pain associated with the stories that have caused you to stop being your Self. You will rarely face them willingly. It hurts. You resist. You point the finger. You say it is them, not me. You believe your pain has been caused by someone, anyone. "They hurt me. They treated me badly. They did this or that."

The stories are never-ending. Your challenge is to stop, look back to your Self, and explore what has caused the pain. What you will discover is that the source of your inner pain is never them, it is always you.

There is a popular idea that there is one perfect person for you. There is one true love for you. But it may not be what you think.

Your one true love is you. You are the love you seek. Once you find your Self, you will know a love that lasts forever.

Love is not limited in any way. You can love everyone and anyone. You can love all people and love them all with the same intensity. Love is love. It is a gift given by the divine. When you open to it, you open to the divine.

True love doesn't begin or end, it is and always was.

You cannot stop loving someone. You can only stop relating to their story.

You were created by love, as love, and for love. Live each day immersed in the love of the divine. It is why you are here. And it is the very source of your well-being.

Try saying it right now. Say it out loud so that anyone who hears you will know you mean it. "I am love."

BE YOUR SELF AND BE WELL!

|||||||||||||||||||||||||||||||||||||||||||||||||||||||||||||||||||||||||||||||||||||||||||||||||

🍃 HEALING EXERCISE

Call Your Self Love

FIND A QUIET PLACE TO SIT WHERE YOU ARE comfortable and undistracted.

Sit quietly and breathe slowly, deeply, and rhythmically. Follow the air as it moves in and out of your body. Notice the way your chest rises and falls with your breath. Allow your Self to become deeply relaxed and fully present as you breathe.

Once you're calm and centered, present and relaxed, move

your attention to your chest and belly. Notice how you feel.

Next, think of a name that is not your own, one you would not like. Use the name you thought of and say, "My name is _____."

Notice how you feel. Pay particular attention to the way you feel in your chest and belly.

If you're like most people, you will feel uncomfortable. You might experience a bad or yucky feeling. You might even feel sick. Calling your Self the wrong name will feel unnatural or bad.

Notice it. Then stop and move on. Breathe until the feeling has passed and you feel present and relaxed again.

Next say, "I am Love."

Notice how you feel in your chest and belly when you call your Self Love.

When I do it, I feel right and I know it's true.

How did you feel?

I recommend repeating this exercise every day until it becomes second nature to think of your Self as Love. Every time you look in a mirror say, "Hello, Love!"

Do some writing or journaling about your experience.

CHAPTER NINE

YOUR WORDS CREATE YOUR LIFE

"Raise your words, not your voice.
It is rain that grows flowers, not thunder."

— RUMI

WORDS ARE POWERFUL. CHOOSE THEM CAREFULLY.

The creator responds as if every statement you make is a prayer or request. Whatever you say focuses the creative power of the divine on the manifestation of what you have asked for.

Be mindful. Your words create your life even when you're not aware of what you're saying.

If the creator were right next to you, would you change the way you talk?

Imagine you're always talking to the divine. Speak words of love, joy, and gratitude. Your life experiences will start to match your words.

Pay careful attention to the ways you speak about relationships and people. Negativity will focus the power of your intention on the negative. Saying negative and judgmental things will strengthen and reinforce negativity toward others. Your relationships will become negative and adversarial instead of open and loving.

Speaking negatively gives energy to the negative and it grows. Before long everything will become negative.

Negativity also creates suffering. The situations and circumstances of your life will become more difficult. Challenges will grow larger. Problems will become insurmountable. And pain will increase.

Reinforce the positive. Focus your attention on it. Start with words that match the world you want to live in.

If you want a life that is peaceful and loving, speak words of peace and love. If you want a life that is satisfying and fulfilling, speak as if that is the life you have.

You'll see it when you believe it. And the more you say it, the more ingrained it will become. The strength of your belief will grow and your life will change to match your belief.

Positive words focus your attention on the positive. They, just like the negative words, focus the creative power of the divine. You ask for the creation of good and good is what you get. The end result is the perception that your life is good. Everything will start to get easier as your life naturally and organically improves.

I experience the power of words in my own life. When I become negative, all I can see are my flaws. Somehow, like magic, they instantly grow and multiply. I see every little flaw in my home, my family, and the world around me. Problems grow like weeds and take over the landscape of my vision. Before long, the only things I can see are terrible problems. Life becomes nothing but problems, ugliness, and suffering.

When I am positive and speak words that are in harmony with my true Self, what I see are all the wonderful and positive things in my life. The flaws and problems magically disappear. My home is a happy, comfortable place. My children are beautiful and amazing. The world is a beautiful and fulfilling place, filled with goodness.

The way the world looks to me has almost nothing to do with the world itself. Nothing in the world actually changes. It's all about me and the way I interact with the world. It's my perception that matters most. The eyes with which I look determine what I see. And my eyes are guided by the way I think and speak.

When you speak positive words, your inner awareness gets focused on the positive. As a result, you will see the positive everywhere you look. When you are positive, the world will look good. And then it feeds back to you and you will become even more positive. It is a spiral that leads either up or down. The direction you travel is dictated by your words.

The divine lives through each and every person. Everyone is an ambassador for the creator and will report back with whatever you say. What do you want the divine to hear about you and your life?

I'm reminded of a Christian biblical saying: "Ask, and it shall be given unto you." You will receive what you ask for.

Take a moment to think about the general tone of the way you talk. What have you been asking for? Is it positive and loving? Or is it negative and judgmental? If your words create your life, what have you been creating? Is it what you truly want?

When people come to see me, I often hear, "I have a bad back; a bad leg; a bad hip."

I want to stop them right there. There's nothing bad about that body part. But by speaking about it that way, they unintentionally turn it into something that is bad. Now they have a much bigger problem than they started with.

If that body part is bad, we probably can't fix it. They're

going to be stuck with it. Labeling something as bad cements it into being bad.

Don't use words recklessly. Say what you mean and mean what you say. Through awareness, you change.

Once you notice how you speak, you can't help but change it. You will choose your words more carefully. You'll want to speak only the truth. You'll say what you mean and mean what you say.

As you change the way you speak, you will accentuate the positive. It will grow and multiply. You will become, on the outside, a more accurate representation of your true Self.

This will have a direct effect on your physical health and well-being. In the words of best-selling author Bernie Siegel, "If I told patients to raise their blood levels of immune globulins or killer T-cells, no one would know how. But if I can teach them to love themselves and others fully, the same changes happen automatically." Your body responds to your positive words and attitude. Better health comes from a positive attitude. And a positive attitude is reinforced by positive, supportive words.

You choose the way you see things. You can focus on the illusion of darkness and thereby see it as real. You can speak words that reinforce it. Through your negative lenses, you have the capacity to see darkness as the absolute truth. If you do, it will absorb all the power you give it. It will grow and grow while you become less and less. Darkness will eventually become your entire world.

You can also choose to focus on the light. Ultimately, it is the truth of life and will completely overpower any darkness you may have created with your negativity. Positive words will shape the lenses through which you see the world. The world will look bright. The light will be all there is to see.

Occasionally patients don't show up for their scheduled

appointments. My first inclination might be to take it personally. I might think, "How rude and disrespectful! My time is valuable! Someone else could have taken that time!"

Then I remember Ann. She and her husband were both patients. They often scheduled back-to-back appointments and came together. One day they didn't show up. And because I had them both on my schedule, I had a big open hole in the middle of my day.

I found my Self getting angry and worked up. I focused on the lost income and the other people who could have taken those times. In that moment, it became all about me.

I called and got no answer. I sat stewing in the pool of my Self-created negativity.

I got a call a few days later. It was Ken, Ann's husband. She had gotten very sick and was in the hospital. They thought she might have leukemia. Then he apologized for missing their appointments.

I felt terrible. I had felt angry and disrespected. I had made the situation all about me and my needs. And the truth was, it had nothing to do with me. I was the one being disrespectful, not them.

That call stopped me in my tracks; it still gives me pause. It's almost never about me. It's only my arrogance that makes it about me.

As this illustrates, you almost always create your own problems and negativity. The darkness you manufacture and see is your own. And it's not real.

Whenever you find your Self getting stuck in negativity and complaints, the challenge is to stop. Stop and remember the negativity is your own creation. The truth is that darkness is only the absence of light. Nothing is real but light.

Reset your perspective by resetting your words. Speak

positive, loving words that turn your focus back to the light. Find gratitude for what you have instead of focusing on what you don't have.

If I had been focused on the light when Ken and Ann didn't show up for their appointments, I might have avoided all my judgment and negativity. Instead of thinking "how rude," I might have wondered what happened instead of getting angry.

Nothing about the situation would have been different. But the way I felt and responded to it would have been. The situation had nothing to do with me, but I made it all about me. In my arrogance, I created the negativity and strengthened the darkness.

Close your eyes for a moment and imagine the world around you and everyone in it is the light of the divine. How does it look and feel?

Carry that image with you. Make it the foundation from which you live and speak.

Speak as if the creator is right there with you. Speak as if you and everyone you know are the light of the divine in human form. Speak as if the creator will give you exactly what you ask for.

The changes you see will be nothing short of miraculous. Speak with a miraculous voice and miracles will follow.

BE YOUR SELF AND BE WELL!

🍃 HEALING EXERCISE

Speak as if You Already Have the Life You Want

What sort of life would you like?

Sit comfortably and breathe deeply with your eyes closed until you are calm, relaxed, and present.

Once you are calm and centered, ask your Self, "What are the top two or three things I want most in my life?"

If they are things and not states of being, ask what having those things will do for you.

For example, you might want a life partner, a husband or wife. Ask what that relationship will bring you that you don't have now? Possible answers are security and intimacy.

It's not the relationship itself you seek. It's the security and intimacy that come with the relationship. This is true of almost every "thing."

Once you have identified the top two or three things you want most, imagine you already have them. Let your Self feel how it feels to have everything you most want.

Do some writing or journaling about your experience. Include the things you want most and how it looks and feels to have them.

Finally, speak as if you already have the perfect life that includes your two or three top desires.

For example, if you want peace and contentment, start saying, "I feel peaceful and content." Write it down. Feel how it feels. Say it as often as possible. Tell everyone you know that you are peaceful and content.

Pay attention to how others respond to you. Notice if you start to experience life differently.

If you catch your Self starting to revert to any negativity, stop and purposely change the way you talk. Speak the life you want.

CHAPTER TEN

FINDING YOUR INNER VOICE

"Before I can tell my life what I want to do with it, I must
listen to my life telling me who I am."
— PARKER J. PALMER

YOUR INNER VOICE IS AN EXPRESSION OF THE life given to you by the divine. It's like a song filled with feelings, sensations, and awareness. All you have to do is find a quiet place to listen. Once you get away from all the noise and distractions, it will be right there.

All things have an inner voice that speaks the language of the divine. But there are no human words that adequately convey that language. Our human language is incapable of fully describing the divine.

To hear your inner voice, you will need to listen for something other than words. You'll need to move your attention from the chatter in your head to the feelings and sensations that exist below your neck.

If you listen to your body, it will guide you to the inner voice of your true Self.

The creator gave you your voice and expects you to use it. Finding your inner voice brings you closer to the divine and guides you in fulfilling your life purpose.

You have a voice, just like everyone else. All people contain the voice of the creator within them. Everyone's voice is important. We need yours just as much as anyone else's.

You are as wise as anyone. Listen for your inner voice and let it be a lighthouse guiding you back to your inner wisdom and essential oneness with the creator. You can be certain that you were made to be you. It isn't a mistake. The creator doesn't make mistakes.

You might think you can't. You might think you are flawed and broken, incapable of expressing the voice of the divine.

The truth is, you are here to be a mouthpiece for the divine in your own, unique way. The world is a lesser place, incomplete without you and your voice. To get on the path of deep fulfillment is to embrace this simple truth. The creator gave you your inner voice. You are here to find it, follow it, and live it.

Your inner voice isn't the one you talk with. And it isn't the voice that speaks in your head. Your inner voice doesn't speak a human language. It speaks with feelings, sensations, and wordless awareness. It's not in your head. It's in your body.

Once you get in touch with the feelings and sensations, you can use your brain to make sense of them. It can help define and give words to what you have felt and known intuitively.

Words will help satisfy the curiosity of your mind. But if you're like me and many of the people I have worked with, you will discover that it is challenging to talk about your inner voice. We don't have the words.

Some people call it intuition. Others, a gut feeling. Some will say they knew it in their heart or felt it in their solar plexus. It doesn't matter what you call it.

What does matter is the awareness that it is your inner voice. It is the one that calls out to you about things that matter.

When you hear it, you will simply know in a way that can't easily be explained.

Have there been times when you knew something was right, even though you couldn't explain it? That sense of "rightness" comes from your inner voice.

There are many tools and techniques you can use to get in touch with your inner voice. Walks in nature, yoga, meditation, prayer, massage, the list goes on and on. No technique is better than another. The best technique is the one you enjoy and will do regularly.

The magic isn't in the technique, it's in you. If you find a technique that works for you, that's the one to use. If you like doing yoga, do yoga. If you like meditating, meditate. The technique is only a tool, an aid to help you find your voice.

The key is to escape the noise of the world and the constant chatter in your head. Our noisy world will cover it up. And the voice in your head will drown it out. Your inner voice, the voice of your true Self, is soft and quiet.

Activities like yoga, meditation, and quiet walks in nature work because they help you to be quiet. And to hear your inner voice, you must be quiet. You need to make it a regular practice.

Your inner voice is the voice of your spiritual identity, your true Self. When you hear it, you hear the voice of the divine speaking through you. The more you listen, the more you will start to become the voice of the divine alive in human form.

That voice is a large part of why you were created. Find your inner voice and you will find your core purpose for being alive. Expressing it increases the divine's presence in the world.

You are not here to be what you think you should be. You are here to be the real you. The voice in your head isn't you and it doesn't express who and what you are. That voice is an imposter that will lead you away from who you are.

Stop for a moment and think of a beautiful flower. That flower is busy being a beautiful flower. It has no other purpose. It doesn't think about what the other flowers might say. It doesn't try to hide its magnificence and be less. It simply blooms.

Be like the flower and bloom. Be unconcerned with anything but being you, the true Self the creator made.

This is how you are meant to be and is why you are here. You are here to be the flower of the divine.

It also gives your body the energy and vitality it needs to be strong and healthy. Your body relies on you. It mimics you so that the more alive you allow your Self to be, the healthier your body will be.

As you express your inner voice, notice what happens to your body. Notice how your body changes. It simply cannot remain unchanged when you let the voice of your true Self sing in the body you occupy. You will begin to look outwardly more and more like the spiritual being you are on the inside.

I see the effects of spiritual presence in my practice all the time. As people find their inner voices and awaken to their true Selves, their bodies change. Once they get in touch with who they are on the inside, their bodies open up and physical healing follows.

A client named Martha had chronic digestive trouble. She lived with abdominal pain and dysfunction for years. She alternated between constipation and diarrhea, rarely experiencing normal bowel function.

After putting up with the pain for years, she finally decided it was time to do something. She made an appointment to see a doctor who told her it was most likely Crohn's disease and gave her a prescription for steroids.

Martha went home and googled Crohn's disease and steroid treatment. She discovered that most of the people who have Crohn's disease and begin taking steroids never get off them. She found a long list of side effects related to steroid use. She thought, "There has to be a better way."

Someone told Martha about me. She didn't know if I could help her, but she knew she didn't want to take steroids. With nothing to lose, she called and made an appointment.

She didn't ask for a healing, at least not on the surface. Martha came to my office thinking I might adjust her spine or give her some herbs or something to help her feel better. Herbs and physical manipulation were about as alternative as she could imagine.

You know how sometimes people will say one thing but mean another? That was my experience with Martha. My gut said she was there for everything I had to offer. I knew she had come for spiritual healing. I followed my gut and I am deeply grateful I did.

My inner voice said, "She needs a healing. Put your hands on her." I listened. That action started major changes.

She called me the very next day to report that her digestive symptoms had flared up. She had diarrhea and cramping abdominal pain that forced her to spend much of the night in the bathroom.

She said, "What is happening to me? You didn't do much of anything during our session. All you did was gently put your hands on me. How could all this be happening when you didn't do anything?"

I was thrilled. I get excited when my clients start having symptoms after I see them. It does require some reassurance, but healing requires the elimination of the old. As the old leaves, symptoms appear in its wake. Symptoms mean that healing is taking place.

After a spiritual healing, anything that is not in harmony

with your true Self must be purged. Your old patterns of sickness and dysfunction are incompatible with your inner voice.

Over the course of our first several months working together, Martha lost about ninety pounds. She wasn't trying to lose weight. She was trying to be her true Self. But in finding her inner voice, she found the capacity to let go and be. Her body followed her lead and let go of the weight.

The most important changes were internal. It all started when she acknowledged that she was backed into a corner. She needed to be willing to see everything about her life in a new way. And, most importantly, she needed to stop believing the stories she had made up about why things were the way they were. These internal changes led to outer changes in the way she lived.

She started a daily practice of quiet morning meditation. She read books with messages of hope and empowerment. Yoga, exercise, time in nature all became important to her. Martha also followed the dietary changes I recommended and used the nutritional supplements I suggested. But, more than anything else, she started listening to her Self instead of staying busy with stories and distractions. Her inner voice provided the encouragement she needed.

Her digestive symptoms cleared up almost completely. She will occasionally experience symptoms as she uncovers another layer of dysfunction that needs to be released. But as soon as she works through whatever has come forward to heal, her symptoms resolve once again.

Martha woke up who she is on the inside. She rediscovered her inner voice and her body changed to mirror her inner awakening. It was a natural and organic reorganization of the molecules of her physical form to more closely match her inner beauty.

If you were to ask her about it today, she would tell you it was all a result of her spiritual awakening. As she found the voice of her true Self, it encouraged her to make the needed changes.

Find your inner voice, the voice of your true Self. Follow its guidance and you, like Martha, will heal. Let your inner voice guide and direct your life. Make it a priority. When you do, your body will change for the better and you will feel deeply satisfied and fulfilled.

Flowers do not limit their beauty out of fear that another flower might be wounded by their audacity. They simply bloom with whatever beauty and glory they were given. You are here to do the same. You don't need to restrict or limit your magnificence. You were created to embody the magnificence you are.

As you find your inner voice, you will find your life purpose and support your body in creating health and well-being at the same time. You are the source of life and health for your body.

Find your inner voice. Let it sing. And be healthy.

If you want to know what to do in life, you must know who you are. And to know who you are, you must find your inner voice and listen carefully. But once you find it, you'll know just what to do.

BE YOUR SELF AND BE WELL!

||||||||||||||||||||||||||||||||||||||||||||||||||||||||||||||||||||||||||||||||||||||||||

🌾 HEALING EXERCISE

Listen to Your Body

Sit comfortably in a quiet place.

Sit however you like to sit. What matters most is that you're alert and not distracted by your posture or your surroundings.

Close your eyes. Breathe deeply and rhythmically. Focus all your attention on your breath. Follow the air in and out of your chest. As you breathe, relax and allow your Self to be fully present.

While continuing to breathe deeply, move your attention down to your feet and ankles. Notice how they feel. Notice the life inside of them. Allow whatever sensations come from them to occupy your entire being. Be fully present with the sensations in your feet and ankles. Listen and let them speak.

Let the life in your feet and ankles move through you and direct you. If you feel like moving, move. If you feel like making a sound, do it. Try to mimic whatever is happening in your feet and ankles.

Next move your awareness to your knees and legs. Do the same thing you did with your feet and ankles. Notice the sensations and what they are saying. Notice if you feel like moving or making a sound. Notice if they are quiet with no sound or movement needed. If you don't feel directed to make a sound or move, simply sit quietly and observe.

Continue to move your attention through your body, taking time to stop at each body part and allow it to speak. Allow this activity to consume your awareness. Let it take over until it is all you are aware of.

What you are doing is listening to your inner voice. It speaks through the feelings and sensations, the life in your body.

At first you might feel awkward or impatient. You might not feel or hear anything. It takes time and practice to get proficient at this exercise. It might take quite a while before you feel or hear anything at all.

If you don't feel or hear anything, simply accept it and move on. It isn't a test. You can't do it wrong. Just notice and keep doing it. Do it every day.

If you're like me, one day when you least expect it, you'll hear something. It might be startling. That event will mark the beginning of something wonderful. You will have contacted your inner voice.

Once you hear it, I'm quite certain you'll want to hear it again. It will probably become very important to you.

Each time you listen and hear your inner voice, you'll be more fully and passionately alive. You'll be contacting and giving a voice to the energy of life the creator placed within you.

Take some time to write or journal about your experience. Include how it felt and what you heard or were aware of. Include anything that comes to you. Write until you feel complete and have nothing else to say.

CHAPTER ELEVEN

HEALTHY SELFISHNESS

"Self-care is not selfish. You cannot serve from an empty vessel."
— ELEANOR BROWNN

DO YOU AND YOUR NEEDS COME LAST, OR FIRST?

Healthy Selfishness is believing you are as important and valuable as anyone else. It's being able to say "I love you" to your Self as easily as you can to anyone else. It's having the courage to make you the most important person in your life.

Are you the most important person in your life? If you are— if you can put your Self first—something amazing will happen. You'll find you're able to give like never before.

The more you prioritize you and make time for your Self, the more you'll be able to give to others. The simple truth is that you can't fill anyone's glass from an empty pitcher. It doesn't mean you always have to say no to others. It doesn't mean you can't give freely and live a life of service.

Healthy Selfishness is about balance. It's about getting re-filled when you're empty. It's about nurturing your own light so that you can light the way for others.

Healthy Selfishness is also about saying yes to your dreams and making them a priority.

Make the choice, right now, to focus on you and your innate creative potential. Say yes to your dreams, as they will bring passion and meaning to your life.

This passion and meaning will fill you with energy and you'll be able to give even more. Pursuing your inner dreams and desires serves the world. It's not selfish in a me-only way. It is Selfish in a way that makes the world bigger and better.

Those inner dreams of yours are a gift from the creator. Following them just might set you on your life's path. And that won't take anything away from anyone else. It will only be helpful and positive.

You have the creative power of life within you. Its potential is limitless. But if you don't say yes to your Self, you will never find it or know it. You have to prioritize your Self to get to know who you are. You must make time for you to find and follow your dreams. If you're always busy giving to everyone else, you won't know your Self. You won't be able to get in touch with your inner dreams, let alone bring them to life.

If there is something you're drawn to, something you really want to do deep down, stop and say yes. Honor the voice of your dreams. Live your passion.

When you say yes, you choose life. When you say no, you choose to give way to apathy and depression.

You're not here to give up and be lifeless and depressed. You're here to be vibrantly alive. Find your passion. Follow your dreams and be all you can be. It is the Selfishness that serves both you and the world simultaneously.

You can follow your dreams and inner desires. You can. I'm giving you permission. You can strive to be all you can be. Not only do you have my permission, the creator undoubtedly wants and expects it.

Following your dreams is the same as following the voice of

your true Self. Pursuing them activates and engages your passion. As a result, you become more vitally alive. You'll rarely feel as alive and energized as when you're following your dreams.

Many people turn away from their dreams and coast through this life, numb and half asleep. I'm sure you see it all around you. It leads to apathy, depression, and the dim light of mediocrity. When you don't prioritize your Self, you close the door on your inner dreams and become just another person coasting along without meaning and purpose.

The abandonment of hopes and dreams lies at the foundation of much of our societal discontent. No dreams means no passion. Depression, lack of contentment, and the inability to find joy in life are all creations of the Self-denial that comes from giving up on what you feel passionate about.

You are not here to be lifeless and depressed. You are not here to try to be someone or something else. You are not here to follow someone else's dreams. You are here to be you. You are here to live with passion and vitality. You are here to follow your dreams and be an inspiration for others.

Your dreams were placed within you by the creator. Healthy Selfishness is choosing to honor the creator's gift and live with passion and meaning.

Prioritize your Self. Say yes to you. Find your inner fire and use it to start fires of passion and meaning all around you. Then watch your world change.

Stop for a moment and imagine the immense creative power of the divine. Now remember that you were created by the very same creative power. Every wonder in the world is also alive inside of you. Find your dreams and cultivate your own creative power.

Choose to take that first step. It doesn't matter what it is. Just take a step. All journeys, short or long, begin with one small step.

It could be as simple as writing something on a scrap of paper or telling a friend how you feel. What matters is that you are saying yes to your dreams. Saying yes to your dreams is the ultimate way of saying yes to your Self. You are saying yes to your Self and yes to the creative power of the divine at the same time.

You might think you could never accomplish your dream. Why even try? But the joy is not in the accomplishment, it is in the pursuit. Simply acknowledging your dreams and becoming open to them sets you on the path of joy.

As Eckhart Tolle says, "Do not be concerned with the fruit of your action—just give attention to the action itself. The fruit will come of its own accord."

Things will appear as they are meant to appear. Put your Self into the steps along the way. Put your heart and soul into whatever you're doing. The final product will be a manifestation of the dreams of your heart and soul.

I used to have business partners. The three of us spent ten years together. It was rewarding in many ways. We all valued a holistic approach to health and healing. Our common goal was to create a clinic that honored body, mind, and spirit, seeing it as the only path to true wellness.

My partners and I worked hard to create a clinic that included a variety of complementary therapies, a true multidisciplinary clinic. We hired massage therapists, body workers, and healers. Everything seemed to be going great. But under the surface, not everything was harmonious.

In our own way, each of us gradually realized that we didn't want to run and manage the business we'd created. We were practitioners focused on healing, not managers focused on the details of the business.

After about four years, we came-to and decided to downsize. It was a big decision that required courage and a degree of healthy Selfishness. We gave everyone notice of our intention to downsize knowing full well that many of them would be out of work. We had to set up in a new location. That meant we had to notify all our clients knowing some of them would never return.

If we focused outwardly on everyone else instead of inwardly on our own dreams, we probably wouldn't have been able to make these changes. And we would have cheated ourselves. In the long run, it probably wouldn't have worked. Something would have had to give.

Sometimes divine guidance takes over and things happen the way they are meant to happen. In the end, we created a clinic that was much better for all of us. We felt energized; we returned to the passion that led us to be healers in the first place. We had more time for clients. Everyone was happier and had more energy to put into the things we loved, which meant our work improved, allowing us to be of greater service. We even made more money.

Healthy Selfishness allows you to follow the path that is right for you even when it might appear to have a negative impact on others.

In some ways it would have been easier to stay with what we had. It was a good business. We provided jobs. But it wasn't "our" clinic, the business of our inner dreams. It was the business we thought we were supposed to create.

The truth is, we weren't happy. We weren't happy because we weren't following our own dreams. We were busy creating what we thought we were supposed to want. And that could never make us truly happy.

Stop for a moment and think of the things you spend most of your time doing. Then ask if they are the way you want to spend your time. Are they what you truly want to do?

If you want to find passion and joy in your life, it must come from you. No one else's dream will ever make you truly happy.

Healthy Selfishness is allowing your Self to be Self-centered and Self-directed. It is the only path to real and meaningful fulfillment. And when you are happy and fulfilled, you will be of far greater service to others. It doesn't mean you don't care about others. It means you care enough about your Self and others to bring your whole being into the relationship.

When the things you choose to do in this life come from your inner Self, they will be perfect. When the motivation for your activities flows forth from you and your innermost desires, they will be just right for you and everyone else. Guided by healthy Selfishness, you'll love what you do and do things that are truly loving.

Imagine a life where almost everything you do is what you truly want to do. Imagine a life that is mostly an expression of love and joy. This life can be yours. All you have to do is be your Self and let your inner voice be the inspiration for your life.

Putting your Self first is not only healthy, it is necessary. It is necessary for you to be the loving and supportive person you want to be. It's not about avoiding being negatively selfish, it's about giving freely from the space of open honesty in your expression of love.

Healthy Selfishness allows you to give from a full cup because you truly want to give. It transforms the idea of giving into simply loving—loving your Self and all others with grace and ease.

BE YOUR SELF AND BE WELL!

≈ HEALING EXERCISE

Find and Live Your Dreams

Do you have dreams you forgot or have given up on? Are there things you always wanted to do that you abandoned because they seemed unattainable or irrational? Did you give up without even trying?

Find a quiet place to sit, breathe, and be. Move your attention from your noisy thoughts to the quiet stillness of your true Self.

Once you're calm and centered, take a moment and go back in time to when you felt deeply passionate and energized by something. Focus on something that existed inside of you and not something from the outside.

For example, you might have found a sporting event or theatrical production inspirational. This exercise isn't about what someone else did. It's about finding what you wanted to do.

Take a moment to go back and get reconnected with the passion and energy of your dreams. Imagine you did whatever you wanted to do. See, in your mind's eye, whatever you wanted to create. Bring it to life inside your Self.

Let your Self feel all the feelings and energy of having realized your inner dreams. You brought your dreams to life. How does it feel?

Next, make a list of steps you can take and things you can do to accomplish your dream. Choose healthy Selfishness and take the steps necessary to make it happen.

Remember the steps along the journey are 90 percent of the joy and fulfillment. Only a very small part lies in the final product.

Walking the path of your dreams is living your dreams.

Spend some time writing or journaling about your experience. Include the details of your dreams and the way you felt when you let your Self have what you wanted.

CHAPTER TWELVE

RELATIONSHIPS ARE MIRRORS

"When you judge another, you do not define them,
you define yourself."
— WAYNE DYER

EVERY RELATIONSHIP IS A MIRROR. WHAT YOU see is either the real you or an imposter, a false you. The purpose of the mirror is to help you see what's blocking you so that you can heal. The mirror shows you one of two things: your true Self or the not-self.

When you live and act as your true Self, the mirror will show you love. Your relationships will reflect your loving nature. They will be delightful, fun, and fulfilling.

When you live and act as the not-self, the mirror will show you pain and judgment. The not-Self will be reflected back to you as disharmony in the relationship.

When your true Self is hidden, love will be lacking. The image you will get from the mirror of your relationships will be the pain of your not-self.

Relationships serve one of two simple purposes. They help you experience the love and joy of being your true Self, or they point out where you have turned away from your Self and blocked love.

Everything you experience in your relationships is either love or an indication that love is lacking. In other words, you are present or you are not. When you're present, your relationships will be loving. When you are not present, your relationships will be difficult and painful.

This truth will change everything you know about your relationships. You will begin to understand they exist for your highest good. Any pain or stress you experience is meant to help you, not to hurt you. Painful relationships are just an indication of your own need to change.

Underneath it all lies the only change that is needed. It is the change that takes place when you return to the love of your true Self. Author and teacher Marianne Williamson calls it "the return to love" and rightly says it fixes every problem.

The mirror shows you what to look for. You might be tempted to look outward and blame the other person. But your job is not to fix the relationship. Your job is to fix your Self. Once you do, the relationship will fix itself. The mirror of your relationships will show you what to look for inside your Self.

The deeper truth is you don't need to be fixed. Your true Self is perfect. You need to explore the source of your inner pain so you can discover it isn't real and return to being your Self.

Once you resolve your inner pain, your relationships will almost magically return to peace. They will, once again, mirror your essential identity as a loving spiritual being.

The thing to remember is that it's all about you. Your relationships serve you by showing you where you have stopped being your Self. Although uncomfortable, your pain and difficulties are gifts that can guide you back to the loving being you're meant to be.

Your relationships follow you. Others respond to who you are and act accordingly. What you get on the outside is a direct result of what's happening on the inside. Hurtful, unloving words and actions can't come from the real you. Those things can only come from your ego or not-self.

When you are not being your true Self, when you are trying to be something other than who you are, you can become cold and unloving. You, like everyone, can do all sorts of hurtful things.

If you are not experiencing love in your relationships, it means you are not present. It's a reminder that you have stopped being your Self. When love is lacking, stop and look to your Self. When and why did you stop being you?

Look inward for the pain and fear that stops you from being your Self. Explore the walls you have built around your heart. These walls keep you locked in and love locked out. They allow the voice of the not-self to take over and rule. And when the not-self runs your life, destruction is going to be the outcome.

Healing comes with inner awareness. As you explore inwardly, you will change outwardly. You will start to remember who you are and once again allow the voice of love to guide and direct your life.

It's rare that much needs to change on the outside. The only fixing that ever needs to take place is simply the dismantling of the story of the not-self and the simultaneous restoration of your true Self.

The not-self is wounded. It thrives on pain and problems. It has no idea what real love is. The not-self is the one who points the finger of blame. "It's them, not me. They hurt me and wronged me. I am an innocent victim. They are the reason I am suffering and in pain."

If you notice your Self pointing the finger and blaming others, stop. Stop and ask, openly and honestly, what you can do to change things. Stop looking at them and look back to your Self.

How might you change to reopen the doors of love and start over?

Real intimacy is only possible when you are present and engaged. No you, no intimacy.

The not-self isn't a real person; it certainly isn't you. The best you can achieve when you're acting as the not-self is create a pseudo-relationship with someone who doesn't see or know the real you. In a pseudo-relationship, the best you can get is pseudo-love.

Every person who comes into your life is there to teach you about your Self. Listen to them and pay attention to how you respond. Remember that they are mirrors for you. If your experience is anything other than joy and love, it is because you have something to discover and learn about your Self.

Your job is not to point the finger. Your job is to take notice. Your job is to recognize what is happening in you and return to your Self.

I experienced a situation that illustrates the ways we create stories about the things that happen around us. Through these stories, we determine the nature of our relationships. Those around us have very little to do with it. We assign meaning to what they do and say.

As I was walking to my car one evening, I heard yelling. A woman was screaming and yelling in anger at a security guard who appeared to be escorting her away from the college campus where I had been teaching. The woman was angry. I could feel the anger expressed through her voice.

I immediately felt anxious; my heart pounded in my chest. All the alarm bells in my body were going off, catapulting me into fight-or-flight mode. I blamed the woman for the way I felt. She was making me scared and anxious. She triggered the alarm.

I wanted to send positive energy to the people involved. If she would stop, I could calm down. At that moment, it hit me, stopping me in my tracks. I stopped walking and stood perfectly still.

I was making her responsible for my own inner state of being.

I took a deep breath and asked my Self these questions: "Why am I feeling this way? Why am I scared and anxious? What is this situation telling me about me?"

It hit me that I could very easily be the one doing the yelling. My not-self is quite capable of anger and the violence that often follows. We all experience moments like these. We all get caught up in the stories we tell ourselves about who we are. We all get overwhelmed by our beliefs about what our experiences mean about us and others. We all have moments where we completely abandon our true Selves in favor of something ugly and violent.

My wanting to send them positive, loving energy was an expression of my own fear and arrogance. And in my fear, I would not be capable of sending positive energy, only more fear.

I had no clue what was happening to the woman. Maybe she was doing what was right for her in that moment. I had no business doing anything other than observing her, and through her, my Self.

I now realize that almost any situation that causes me to react violently does so because it exposes my inner wounds. My anger is a deflection. It is a protective mechanism I use to turn my attention away from my inner pain.

It's easier to blame someone else than own up to my own issues. I feel far less vulnerable when I go on the attack. But attacking is not loving. Love is the energy that heals.

I realized then that the woman who was screaming and yelling was almost certainly in a place of great pain. With that realization, I moved from fear and anxiety into acceptance. I felt compassion for the woman.

If you find your Self responding in anger, stop, take a breath, and ask what you're afraid of.

We all carry wounds, deep and traumatic, that will be triggered by our life experiences. Life pokes at our wounds through our relationships. This is when you will lash out in anger. It is rarely about someone else. It is almost always a response to having your inner pain exposed.

The closer and more intimate the relationship, the more pain it will likely provoke. In the midst of it all, the challenge is to remember that it is exposing the pain that already existed inside of you. Instead of running away, move closer to the pain and you will open the doors to healing and freedom.

When the mirror reflects pain, don't go on the attack and fight back. Healing begins with the willingness to be vulnerable and move into your pain. All that is not love will melt away in the presence of love. Hurtful, violent behavior, when confronted with love, is transformed.

It has been said that time heals all wounds. But that is not quite right. Time allows us to bury and forget our wounds. The pain diminishes, but that is not healing. The wound remains alive and well wherever we've buried it.

It is love that heals all wounds. It is the unconditional love provided by the loving presence of another that allows us to truly heal. When we return to the love we are, the light of creation shines on our wounds. In that light, they cease to exist.

Almost every experience of pain and difficulty you encounter in your relationships is, in truth, a loving expression of the greatest magnitude. The pain you feel is almost always your own. It is the pain of living as something other than who you are. The pain is love come to call you home to your Self.

BE YOUR SELF AND BE WELL!

🍃 HEALING EXERCISE

Find the Root of Your Judgments

Sit quietly and breathe deeply until you are calm and present, centered in your Self.

When you are ready, think about a difficult or painful relationship. Allow all the feelings and judgments that are part of the relationship to come to the surface. Feel them as if you have just had a difficult interaction with that person.

How do you see them? How would you describe them? How do they act? What wrongs have they committed? How have they hurt you?

Allow anything that is important in that relationship to come to you. Let it all come forward.

Write down all your feelings and judgments about them. Start each one with "they." For example, "They are cold and unreachable," or, "They don't listen."

Next change your statements. Replace every "they" with "I" or "I am." For example, "They don't listen" becomes "I don't listen."

Relationships are mirrors. The way you judge others is exactly what you fear is true about your Self.

Next, explore the ways you have acted out your "I am" statements.

Finally, ask if it truly was them that caused your pain. How could you take responsibility for your Self and your actions? How could you start over and begin to change the nature of the relationship?

Take some time to write or journal about your experience. Include the steps you're going to take to bring your Self back into the relationship and restore the love that heals.

CHAPTER THIRTEEN

YOU AND YOUR MIND

"Your ego is your soul's worst enemy."
— RUSTY ERIC

AS WEIRD AS IT MIGHT SEEM, THAT VOICE IN YOUR head isn't yours. That voice comes from your ego or mind. It doesn't come from the real you. Your voice comes from your chest and belly. You speak with feelings and sensations, not words. It often expresses as a simple knowing or awareness, what some people call intuition.

You can listen to what your mind says. It's a little bit like listening to another person, just one who can speak inside your head. The more you do it, the more apparent it will become that the voice in your head is not who you are. You'll notice it says things you disagree with and don't believe. There can be a stark contrast between you and the things your ego says. Noticing the differences will help you appreciate that the voice in your head is not who you are.

Once you understand the difference between the voice of your ego and the voice of your true Self, you hold the key to peace and well-being.

The judgments of your ego will create stress and anxiety while your true Self is always calm and peaceful.

You love and accept. You seek intimacy and connection. Love is the guiding force for your true Self.

Your mind judges and rejects. It doesn't understand love at all. It looks only for the differences that create separation. Cold, hard facts are the mind's guiding force. If your mind can't explain something, it discards it.

You live and act from awareness. The simpler the better. You just know, even when you can't explain it.

Wisdom is a natural part of who you are. The creator placed that wisdom inside of you. It allows you to distinguish between good and bad, love and not love. You can feel it when something is not love, not right.

Your mind searches for knowledge, the more the better. It endlessly gathers facts and figures, storing them for later use. It then uses the numbers to reinforce its judgments.

To your mind, love doesn't exist. The best your ego can do is consider the idea of love. It has no appreciation or understanding of love at all. And because of that, love is something to be wary of to your mind, something you can't trust.

Once you have made up your mind, it is unlikely you will change it. You'll hold fast to your beliefs and reject almost any information that contradicts them. There is nothing wise about those beliefs. To a great degree, they only control and limit what you can do and who you can be.

You can know next to nothing and still be very wise because wisdom comes from your inner spiritual awareness. It has very little to do with knowledge. Inner wisdom allows you to be fluid and flexible, responding successfully to life as it unfolds.

Wisdom allows you to see beyond the details of the big picture. It allows you to have an inner awareness of whether something is an expression of love or not.

I experience the contrasting voices of wisdom and knowledge in my practice all the time.

My education was all about the facts and figures. As a student, my job seemed to be to memorize everything I could. Quite frankly, it was overwhelming. There's more information out there than anyone can ever know. No one could possibly memorize it all. But we tried.

The idea was that to be a good doctor, you had to learn it all. The more you knew, the better you were going to be at helping people. Being a doctor seemed to be about knowing everything. We students were busily trying to be human supercomputers.

Making the transition from student to doctor was not easy. As a student, everything was clear-cut, black and white. Then I finished school and quickly discovered that being a student and being a doctor are completely different. I discovered people are endless shades of gray.

Lives are complicated and complex. People are much more than facts and figures. Almost nothing is as clear-cut or black and white as it is in the textbooks.

Messy lives filled with emotion are the norm. Every problem has multiple overlapping factors. Even with all my knowledge, I realized I didn't know much of anything. How was I ever going to help anyone?

Fortunately, I had a mentor. The time I spent with her was invaluable. I found myself almost constantly astonished by the things she would say to people. Over and over again, I asked, "How did you know that? Where did you learn that?"

Patients would come in with neck pain and she would ask about their marriages. It would open the door for those people to admit they weren't happy but held it all in. I wasn't taught to ask about someone's marriage to help neck pain!

Or a person would complain about an issue with the throat or thyroid gland. The next thing I knew they'd be having a conversation about the things that person wanted to say but couldn't. What? I was lost and confused a lot. Thankfully, the lightbulb of understanding gradually lit up.

I gradually started to understand that she hadn't learned those things in school. She went back to school as an adult in pursuit of a second career. Her wisdom came from the life she had lived. It came from inside of her, not from school.

She had lived a rich life and learned much. Above all, she had learned to trust her inner wisdom and use it in her practice.

The things she knew that allowed her to connect with people and help them came from the wisdom of life. No intellectual book learning can even begin to compare with the wisdom of life.

I realized that if I was going to be a great doctor, I had to put what I'd learned in school on the back burner. It wasn't that the information from my education wasn't useful; it was. But most of the really great stuff doesn't come from memorizing facts and figures. The great stuff comes from the wisdom of life. And no matter how many facts you memorize and how much you know, you won't be able to bring that into practice without using your inner wisdom to guide you.

This experience of seeing the vast difference between knowledge and wisdom was part of what helped facilitate my awakening. To do what I wanted to do and help people with the things that matter most, I had to move beyond the limitations of my mind and into the wisdom of my true Self. To access that wisdom, I had to be present. I had to wake up to the truth of who I am and allow my inner voice to be louder than the voice in my head.

I'm certain you know what I'm talking about. You've probably had experiences where you knew something was right or wrong even though you couldn't explain it. Or an experience of knowing someone was behind you even though you didn't hear or see anyone. That awareness comes from your inner wisdom. It is the voice of your true Self, and it knows things your mind can't grasp.

My mind still says, "This is low back pain, focus on a physical diagnosis and get the job done."

But my inner awareness reminds me that, "This is a person with lower back pain. You need to get to know the person, not just treat the symptoms. Ask about the details of your patient's life; the real answer to the pain probably lies there."

As I move closer and develop a deeper, more intimate relationship with the patient, the hidden truth becomes clear. And that awareness changes everything.

Spend some time observing the voice in your head. See if you can identify things it says that you know are not true. It will help you cultivate your discernment. The more you observe your thoughts, the better you will become at differentiating between you and your mind. Once you start to hear things you don't believe, you will know without doubt that the voice in your head isn't you.

Once you see this, you can never un-see it. It will expose the voice in your head for what it is: an imposter. In that moment, you will be free. You'll be able to stop believing and acting from everything your thoughts say. You can relax and be present in your body where the inner awareness that leads to love exists.

Take a moment to relive a time when you were deeply in love. Go back to that experience. Bring back all the feelings and energy of being deeply in love.

How did it feel? Did your heart respond? Did it affect your mood and energy?

Now consider this: If you had never been in love, would you know what it felt like just by thinking about it?

Being in love and thinking about love are two very different things.

Your mind might be able to talk about love, but it has no idea what it is or feels like. And because it can't understand it, it fears and judges it.

On the other hand, the real you, your true Self, is love. Love is the language of your true Self.

There will always be conflicts between you and your mind or ego. Your mind will always judge and criticize you because it can't comprehend who and what you are. Once you begin to understand and accept this, you can stop believing all the negative garbage your ego says about you. It's just trying to protect itself from something it finds terrifying.

You'll be able to relax and be the loving wisdom you are, no matter what your brain has to say about it.

When you're thinking, you're judging. When you're being, you're loving.

BE YOUR SELF AND BE WELL!

🌿 HEALING EXERCISE

Let Love Guide Your Relationships

Find a quiet, comfortable place to sit.

Close your eyes and breathe deeply and rhythmically, allowing your Self to relax and be fully present.

When you're ready, take a moment to think of someone you know well and have a conflict with.

Think of the situation and all the feelings that go along with it. Notice the things you think about the other person, especially the judgments. How would you describe that person and the situation?

Take a moment to jot it down. For example, the person is closed-minded and shallow, or doesn't listen.

Next, set your notes aside and return to deep breathing until you feel calm and relaxed once again.

As you breathe, move your attention to your heart. Breathe into it, allowing all your awareness to be focused on your heart.

Now ask your Self how you feel in your heart about this person. For example, I love this person.

Jot that down.

Make note of the difference between the things you've written. Your first list is probably negative and judgmental. The statements probably all start with "this person is." Your second list is likely short and sweet with the statements beginning with "I."

Ask your Self how your heart would choose to interact with the other person. Ask your Self what love would do.

Finally, spend some time writing or journaling about your experience. Include the contrast between the way your ego thinks of the person and the way your heart feels about the person. What would you do if you allowed your heart to lead the way instead of your mind?

CHAPTER FOURTEEN

MAKE LOVE THE CURRENCY OF YOUR LIFE

"Love is the great miracle cure.
Loving ourselves works miracles in our lives."
— LOUISE HAY

WHICH DO YOU VALUE MORE: LOVE OR MONEY?

Which do you spend more time pursuing: love or money?

If you're like most people, you value love over money. But, like most people, you probably spend way more time trying to get money than foster love.

No matter how much money and material wealth you have, in the end it won't matter. When you come to the end of your time on Earth, you will return home empty-handed.

So, what is your money and stuff worth to you? What do you sacrifice and miss out on while you're chasing after money and material possessions?

I know when I'm busy working, I'm not with my children. They grow up in my absence. And I will never recover the time and experiences I miss. No amount of money can begin to make up for the joy I get from their hugs and smiles.

When I'm caught up in the pursuit of bigger and better, I

only see what I don't have. I become blind to all I do have. Instead of feeling grateful, I feel jealous. All I know is lack. All I feel is the unsatisfied longing for things that will never actually fulfill me.

Money isn't truly fulfilling. It's nice, but what I crave more than anything is the love I feel in my heart when I'm present and engaged with those I care about.

If you're like most people, you work long and hard for your money. But it's a poor substitute for living and loving. There's just no love to be found in a dollar bill. The wonderful thing about love is that it's everywhere and it's free. All you need to do is be open to it.

I'm not saying money and possessions are bad; they're not. Money is useful; it has its purpose. It's very difficult to get by without it.

But, how much do you need? At what point does money stop serving you and you start serving money? Have you become a slave to your possessions?

Money and possessions can become an impediment to being the love you are. You begin to live for the money you can make instead of the love that satisfies your heart and soul. Before long, you start to hoard what you have accumulated. Greed replaces generosity and open, loving compassion.

I learned a valuable lesson when I got in trouble with money. I hadn't been out of school very long, and four years of chiropractic college is very expensive. I was a new doctor with a student loan payment the size of a mortgage and no house to show for it. I was drowning in debt and, even though I didn't realize it at the time, it was squeezing the life out of me.

I looked at other successful doctors. They seemed to have plenty of money and the wonderful possessions that went along with it. I looked at their lives and said, "I want that."

But I wasn't looking at them. I was only looking at the outside, the superficial. I saw the material wealth and looked past everything else. I also forgot that none of them were brand-new, fresh-out-of-school doctors like me. They had worked hard and paid their dues.

I spent my time trying to model my Self and my life after them. I did what they did. I said what they said. I dressed like they dressed. None of it was me.

I was play-acting, doing what I thought I was supposed to do. But because it didn't come from me, it didn't have any real passion or power behind it. I was little more than an empty shell living for the artificial material world instead of spiritual meaning and fulfillment.

I joined forces with a couple partners and we created a big, beautiful clinic. It was spectacular. It was big and fancy. We were living large, giving every impression of material success. We gave holiday bonuses. We even rented a limo and took everyone to dinner and the theater.

I always wanted a lake cabin so I purchased some lakeshore property. One lot wasn't enough. I had to have three.

It was great fun for a while. Then the bills started to mount up. There wasn't enough coming in to match what was going out. I ended up in bankruptcy.

I felt like a complete and total failure. I had no idea who I was or what my purpose was. My Self-worth was entirely based upon the external. I thought life was all about money and material wealth. If I had enough money, I would surely be happy.

The truth was that I was lost and miserable. I stayed that way until I found my true Self and remembered what was truly important and fulfilling. And it's not money.

In retrospect, the crash was inevitable. I had no inner life. I didn't even know what that was. I needed a shock, a massive, attention-getting explosion. So, life, guided by the loving hand of the divine, provided just what I needed. I lost everything and was brought to my knees.

Let my experience be a lesson for you. Ask your Self where your focus is. Are you working to live or living to work? Are you seeking satisfaction and fulfillment in money and material possessions? Is it working?

Sometimes life challenges us to get our attention. My bankruptcy helped save me. It wasn't a failure or loss. It was a gift. What I was given has completely changed my life.

You can do the same. And you can do it without waiting for a disaster to strike. Choose to look today. Take an honest look at your life and the things you spend your time with. Do they nurture and satisfy your soul or do they distract you from being who you are?

You might find the real you needs very little in the form of money and possessions. It might be nice to drive a fancy car or live in a big house. It might be fun to have a fast boat or a new pair of skis. But they do next to nothing for your heart and soul.

The real you, the spiritual being created by the divine, seeks to experience life and the deep fulfillment of love. Money and possessions are almost unnecessary. How much of your life are you willing to give up for things that do little for your true Self?

Stop for a moment and think of the things you spend your money on. Are they things you need or are they things you want?

There are things your true Self wants, but they're not actually things. What you want on the inside can't be bought and sold. It's the love and deep fulfillment that comes from knowing your essential oneness with the divine's creations.

There is nothing more satisfying or fulfilling than knowing where you and everyone else came from. Sharing that awareness is what life is all about. But if you forget that, the trouble starts.

When you forget, you'll start looking outward, searching for the magical thing that will satisfy your inner desires. But your inner desires cannot be satisfied by anything on the outside. What you seek is love and meaning.

Have you ever made a purchase, only to discover that it didn't satisfy you in the way you expected? Maybe you got exactly what you thought you wanted. But your inner feeling of emptiness and desire was still there, left untouched and unsatisfied. Why did that happen?

Have you found that almost as soon as you make a purchase, your sights are set on something else, something new and better? Where does that desire for bigger and better come from? And where does it end?

The truth is, it has no end. It is an endless wheel of unsatisfied desire and wanting. There is no end because we're chasing something that doesn't exist outside of us.

Once you know who you are, where you came from, and why you're here, you'll feel content. The divine has given you everything you need.

Money does nothing for your soul. This is the simple, yet shockingly powerful secret of true fulfillment that most of us have lost touch with. Because of this, we're no longer human beings, we're human "doings," frantically chasing a nonexistent dream.

Exhausting your Self chasing the dream of material wealth does not support health and well-being. The tremendous stress of chasing after money often leads to an early grave.

Health and well-being are supported by a sense of inner peace and contentment. And that can only come from contacting your true Self and relaxing into being who you are. Once you know your real purpose in life is to be your Self and feel love, you'll hold the key to everything you've ever wanted.

You were made by love, as love, and for love. Love is the only thing that will truly satisfy your soul. Make it your life's mission to live fully and love deeply.

Love is the currency of a deeply fulfilling life.

BE YOUR SELF AND BE WELL!

|||||||||||||||||||||||||||||||||||||||||||||||||||||||||||||||||||||||||||||||||||||

🍃 HEALING EXERCISE

Do You Need It or Want It?

Find a quiet, comfortable place to sit and breathe deeply. By now you're probably quite good at it!

Close your eyes and breathe deeply and rhythmically. Breathe deeply until you feel calm and centered, relaxed and present.

When you feel ready, turn your thoughts to something you've been thinking about buying. The more it costs, the clearer and more powerful this exercise will be.

Sit with the item for a little while, imagining what it might do for you.

Next, ask your Self, "What will this item do for the real me? Is it something I truly need or is it something I just want?"

Keep in mind that real needs are things you can't live without, like food, shelter, air, and water.

If the item you've been thinking about buying is a want and not a need, where does that wanting come from?

Ask your Self, "Why do I want it? What will it do for me?"

Keep in mind that you are a spiritual being that thrives on love, not money and material possessions. Follow your desire down to its source. Let your Self know what it is you actually want. Is it the item itself? Or are you trying to use that thing as a substitute for love.

Do some writing or journaling about your experience.

Lastly, make a list of the things you spend your money on. Go through the list, one item at a time, asking if it is a need or a want.

Then, make a "needs" list and a "wants" list. Put everything in its appropriate category.

Could you get by without some things?

Money is a symbol. It represents the time and energy you have invested. Finally, ask how much of your life you are willing to give up to get things you don't need.

CHAPTER FIFTEEN

CONFLICT AND PEACE

"You find peace not by rearranging the circumstances of your life,
but by realizing who you are at the deepest level."
— ECKHART TOLLE

CONFLICT. IT'S ALL AROUND YOU. IT'S PRESENT in other people and situations. They draw you in. If you allow it, you can get lost in it.

But maybe you're not the innocent bystander you'd like to think you are. Maybe the world you experience reflects your own inner state.

Could the conflict you experience in the world be an outward manifestation of the conflict you carry inside your Self? Could the world mirror your own inner conflict?

When you are conflicted, the world will become a place of conflict. Conflict in the world around you is a signal, a clear indication you have an inner conflict that needs to be explored and resolved.

When you experience conflict, instead of engaging with it, stop and look inward.

If you want to experience a peaceful world, you must find it inside your Self. Peace starts with you. When you are peaceful, the world will mirror your inner peace.

Have you heard you need to fight for peace? The idea is if you fight hard enough, you can force the world to be peaceful. If you fight against conflict, conflict will end. It sounds good, doesn't it? Unfortunately, it doesn't work.

You can't create peace by fighting. They're polar opposites. Fighting only strengthens conflict. When you're caught up in the fight, peace is lost. The more you fight, the more conflict gains a foothold and grows.

It also places your focus outside of your Self. You end up trying to solve an inner problem with an external solution. When you try to force the world to change without changing your Self, it never works.

As the spiritual leader Mahatma Gandhi said, "You must be the change you wish to see in the world."

Through sheer force of effort, you might be able to create a temporary change in the world. You might be able to temporarily suppress the conflict. But, as long as you continue to hold onto your own inner conflict, conflict will always come back. And when it returns, it will be bigger and stronger than ever.

Fighting against conflict only strengthens it.

To change things, you need to see the conflict as a message meant for you. It might come as a shocking situation you experience like a punch to the gut. It grabs your attention, making it impossible to turn away. That is the challenge of conflict. You're going to want to get involved.

Choosing to not engage is the only peaceful answer. Even when the voice in your head screams at you to join the fight, you must ignore it.

When conflict arises, stop and look inside. There is something you need to resolve.

The conflict will exist inside of you as judgments, negative feelings, and sensations of pain. Stop and notice how you're feeling and what you're thinking. Ask your Self, "Why do I feel this way? What do I really want? Why do I want to fight back?"

It's likely you have opposing beliefs. Their presence will create an internal civil war. If you hang on to both sides, there can't be any peace. Something must give.

If you can get to the bottom of your feelings and beliefs, if you can discover where they came from, you will have the awareness you need to begin resolving your inner conflict.

Your inner conflict will be like what you see in the world around you. The world's mirror is turned toward you. If you have the courage to look, you will undoubtedly find some powerful Self-judgments. Could it be that the world is showing you that you are mad at your Self?

If you experience fighting, look for fighting. If you experience angry yelling, look for anger. Be open to wherever your feelings and sensations lead you. They all need to be given a voice. Peace will naturally return as the conflict is resolved.

Remember, the real you is always peaceful. Any conflict you feel does not come from the real you. Return your awareness to your true Self and you will rediscover your peace.

As you explore your judgments and negativity, you will eventually come to a place where you can see they are untrue. It may be a kinesthetic experience that might not make sense to your brain. Yet you will know it in a way that cannot be denied.

People sometimes refer to it as an "aha moment." It's a moment of inner clarity and brilliance that allows you to perceive the truth in a new way. The light bulb turns on and you suddenly understand.

It will, at first, appear to be about the world around you. You will undoubtedly see fighting, ugliness, and conflict. You will want to go out and change it. You'll want to go to war to make the fighting stop. It's a natural reaction.

The challenge is to notice this and then choose to say, "No, I am not going to join the fight." In the heat of the moment, when the whole world seems to be embroiled in conflict, you need to look away. You need to take a deep breath and remember that it's about you. Look to your Self. The solution to the problem will be there.

Your power lies in returning to your own inner peace. And your inner peace is powerful. It has more power than anything else you could do to create peace in the world.

This is because the world responds to you. When you are present as your true Self, you will bring your peace into the world. The world around you will reflect your inner peace and become peaceful.

The martial art judo means "gentle way." When practicing judo, a person doesn't attack or resist an opponent. The object is to adjust to, and evade, an attack. As you move with an attack, the aggressor will lose his balance and power. In the state of reduced power, the more powerful opponent can be subdued.

When the world around you seems to be on the attack, practice judo. Instead of resisting, move with it. Step aside and allow the inertia of the conflict to carry it away from you. Over time the conflict will dissipate, and the attack will ultimately be abandoned.

The immense power of inner peace was illustrated by the life of Nelson Mandela. He was a black man living in apartheid South Africa. The light-skinned people in power blamed those of color for all their problems.

Mandela was persecuted and imprisoned for decades. It could have been very easy for him to become deeply angry and bitter. The bitterness could have consumed and destroyed him. He could have become no better than his captors.

Instead, he stayed present. He stayed true to himself and

focused on honest forgiveness and loving compassion. After decades in prison, instead of coming out a broken man, he came out whole. He emerged from prison with incredible strength, the strength of his own spiritual presence. He learned to love and forgive. He harnessed the immense power of his own inner peace and used it for great good.

Nelson Mandela became a bright light of peace, transforming an entire country, and became a world leader. You can be like Nelson Mandela. You can be the peaceful center of your own world.

In the past, you've probably overreacted to something someone said or did. It might have been something small. But you exploded. What happened? Was it really about the situation?

The anger that erupts from inside often has little to do with the other person. That person is simply a convenient target. The anger and conflict that was already there inside of you is triggered. So much of the conflict in the world has nothing to do with the present situation. It is an expression of old wounds.

The anger you bury doesn't die. It grows and multiplies. It lives on inside of you getting bigger and stronger. When it does come out, and it will, it's more ferocious than ever. Someone might cut you off on the highway and you feel like killing whoever it was.

This reminds me of my interactions with the baristas at the coffee shop where I like to do my writing. When I am present as my true Self and peacefully order a cup of coffee, I have the most wonderful interactions. We chat and connect. They smile and tell me about themselves. It's lovely. If I bring old anger with me to the counter, I act very differently. My true Self is hidden. I don't smile. I'm short, harsh, and not particularly pleasant.

To their credit, the baristas are generally courteous. But it's not because that's the way they want to respond to me. It's because they are working and are expected to treat customers well. They put on a happy face and do their job. But the energy is vastly different than what I experience when I'm present and engaged as my true Self.

Their response is not about them, it's all about me. I get what I ask for. My negative energy is what they respond to. They become a mirror of my lack of presence and gently remind me I have something to work on.

Underneath it all is a human being who just wants to be loved and accepted for who they are, no different than me. There is no situation that changes this. The roles we play and the jobs we do don't change the fact that we all just want to be seen and loved for who we are.

Experiment with this in your own life. Be an observer of your interactions. Watch carefully and notice how others respond to you. Observe how others respond when you are peaceful and engaged. Notice how people respond to you when you are preoccupied, distant, or angry.

When people heal and live as who they were created to be, everything that isn't peaceful will simply cease to exist.

When you heal and stay fully present no matter your surrounding conflicts, you will engage with others from a space of love. Your loving-kindness and peaceful presence will have a profound effect on the world around you. Peace creates peace.

BE YOUR SELF AND BE WELL!

❧ HEALING EXERCISE

Find the Source of Your Anger

Think of a time you were angry and allowed your Self to lash out at another. Take a little time to relive the conflict.

How did the other person respond to your angry outburst? By getting angry and fighting back?

People will usually respond to anger with anger of their own. The energy of your anger feeds theirs, like throwing gas on a fire. Once the fire is raging, it consumes everything. In that moment, you likely won't remember why you were angry in the first place.

Go back to that situation. Can you remember why you were angry? Was it really about the person you reacted to? Or was that person just a trigger for something already alive inside of you?

On the surface it may seem to be all about the other person. But, if you can look below the surface, you may find something surprising. It probably wasn't about anyone else. That person was just a convenient target.

When you lash out in anger, what you really want is love. You feel hurt or wounded. But admitting you feel hurt seems vulnerable and risky. Instead of being honest, you go on the attack.

Set the experience aside for a moment. Sit quietly and breathe deeply. Breathe until you feel calm, relaxed, and centered. Breathe until you return to peace.

Once you are calm and centered, ask your Self, "Did I really want to lash out in anger or did I just want to be loved?"

Now, imagine the situation again, but this time the fighting never happened. Instead of getting mad, you let down your guard, admitted you felt hurt, and asked for love.

How do you feel?

Spend some time writing or journaling about your experience. Include ways you might bring your new awareness into your relationships.

CHAPTER SIXTEEN

ENERGY AND HEALING

"Miracles do not, in fact, break the laws of nature."
— C. S. LEWIS

ENERGY MEDICINE AND SPIRITUAL HEALINGS can seem pretty weird. I certainly thought so. Then I started to experience things I couldn't explain, things that didn't make sense but were too real to disregard. I suddenly found my Self in a position where things I thought and believed no longer fit my experiences. I had to either deny my experiences or take a new and different look at things. I had to reexamine the beliefs that held me back.

I found I had to change the way I thought about things. I gradually moved from a closed-minded, judgmental view to an open-minded, accepting perspective. Once I changed my thinking, my experiences no longer seemed so odd. All it takes is a small shift in perspective and healings start to make sense. Energy medicine and healings aren't weird at all; they're completely natural.

It doesn't connect if you think the healing is done to you. The truth is, no one can heal you. You must want it and choose it for your Self. It starts and ends with you.

Healing energy comes from the inside, not the outside. It's not what someone does to you. It's how you respond. Healing is what happens when you come forward and allow the power of your inner spirit to do the work.

You were born with the power to heal. It's inside you. It is a gift from the creator, part of who you are. That is where healing energy comes from. It can't be seen and you can't touch it. You may not be able to measure it or define it. Yet, like the creator, its existence is undeniable.

When others help you heal, it's because they were able to draw you out to do the healing. They help. You heal. You respond to what they do and say. You respond to their touch. You come forward and the energy of your true Self flows into every part of your body. It is the divine energy of life that does the healing.

The divine energy of life is in you. It comes from the creator. It is the same energy that brings every life form into being. There is nothing it cannot do and no problem it cannot fix. It is so massive and powerful, it's hard to comprehend. And you can access that power any time you want.

When you shift your thinking, it starts to make sense. Of course, you can heal. Of course, there's healing energy. It can't be any other way. All you have to do is step out of the way and let the healing power of the divine work its magic.

All healers are able to help others heal because they assist others in finding their own inner power. Unaided by the power of the divine, a healer can do almost nothing. But with the power of the divine, miracles can become commonplace.

One of my former mentors sometimes jokingly said, "I don't know. I just work here." I didn't fully appreciate it at the time, but I have come to understand the truth of that statement. I often feel the same way.

My job is to resist the temptation to interfere. When I try

to do what I think needs to be done, I usually get in the way. My interference limits the healing. I must step out of the way and allow a power far greater than me to call the shots. If I can do that, I can help.

That's why I just work here. My job is to allow the wisdom and power of the divine to take charge and do the healing.

If you can access the healing power the creator placed inside you, you can heal anything.

The essence of healing and empowerment is discovering you already have the answer to your problems. It's housed inside you. Once you know that you have the solution to your problem, everything changes. Your power is restored, and healing takes place naturally and organically.

Time and time again, I've watched as people discover they already know just what to do. Their postures change. They relax. Their breathing slows and deepens. They breathe a deep sigh of relief as they let go of the restrictions that blocked their healing. This is when the magic happens.

The creator hasn't left you alone and powerless. You have been given everything you need. My job, and the job of all healers, is to help you facilitate your own healing.

You can do it. If you keep looking inward, you will eventually begin to see through the fog. You may not always like it, but once you see the truth about what needs to change, you will heal.

Healing energy can be powerful and at times confusing. It can even feel bad. If you're sensitive and aware, you've probably felt "negative energy."

Sensitive people may fear what they think of as negative energy. Something feels wrong, and it makes them feel like they need to protect themselves.

Have you ever felt that sense of wrongness, that feeling of negative energy? How have you reacted?

How do you react any time you're afraid?

If you're like most people, you put up walls and barriers. You do this to separate your Self from the threat. The walls and barriers help you feel safe, cocooned in your own little space.

I'd like you to think again about those walls and barriers.

Do they really keep you safe? Do you even need protection? If so, what are you protecting your Self from?

Once you isolate your Self behind your walls and barriers, you become vulnerable. Your walls keep as much in as they keep out. All you succeed in doing is cutting your Self off from life. Ironically, your attempts to protect your Self only make you weaker and more vulnerable.

What if negative energy didn't exist? What if negative energy was nothing more than a lack of real energy, a void? Would you need to protect your Self from it?

Negative energy is just the absence of love. It's like the darkness that is simply the absence of light. Turn on the light and the darkness disappears. Turn on the love and the negative energy disappears. It disappears because it never existed in the first place.

The absence of love feels icky and repulsive. But that doesn't mean it has any real power. It is only an emptiness, a void calling out for love. Fill it with love and it ceases to exist.

You don't need to protect your Self because there's nothing to protect your Self from. It feels wrong to you because you're a being of love. It makes you afraid because you don't understand it. Give it the love it needs and you will only have positive energy.

Instead of calling it "negative energy," try calling it "love-me energy." Any time you encounter it, step toward it instead of away from it. Fill it with your loving presence and it will cease to exist.

It is precisely when you find your Self afraid and wanting to run away from the darkness that the world most needs your light, the energy of your spiritual presence. Draw upon all the love you have flowing through you and extend it into the emptiness. The emptiness will no longer be empty. It will be filled with love.

If you can stay present, you will stay in contact with your essential power. It is the power of love. And it can instantly transform all darkness. The light comes on and the darkness vanishes. Love returns and transforms everything.

Love is the ultimate healing energy. It's what you seek and resonate with because you are love.

What you think of as "positive energy" is your awareness of the love inside of you and others. Your true Self rises and responds to the love in every form of creation. You call it positive because it feels absolutely right.

Nothing feels more positive or right than the energy of loving presence. You, and all people, are drawn to love more strongly than anything else. Love attracts love; light attracts light.

There really is only one energy and it's all positive. It is the essence of energy medicine. It is the power behind all healings. It is the loving energy of the divine, and there is nothing it cannot heal.

Healing energy is absolutely real. It is the energy of love that is alive inside of you. It is a gift from the creator that can heal anything and everything.

BE YOUR SELF AND BE WELL!

❦ HEALING EXERCISE

You Can Heal

Find a quiet, comfortable place where you can sit undisturbed.

Close your eyes. Breathe deeply and rhythmically, following the air as it moves in and out of your body. Your only purpose is to breathe and be.

Allow all your attention to be focused on your breath and your body. Breathe until you feel calm, relaxed, and centered within your Self.

When you feel ready, say the following statements. Allow your Self time to resonate with each statement before moving on to the next one.

"I was born with the power to heal."

"The healing power of the divine is alive inside of me and it is infinite."

"Healing energy is the energy of love. And because love is who I am, nothing can stand in my way."

Allow the truth of these statements to resonate throughout you and your body. Allow the healing power of the divine to fill every cell. Allow anything that is not in harmony with this truth to release out of your body and fade away.

Notice how you feel.

Do some writing or journaling about your experience.

I recommend doing this exercise every day. Do it until it becomes part of who you are.

CHAPTER SEVENTEEN

BE GREAT AND TIMELESS

"Our deepest fear is not that we are inadequate. Our deepest fear is that
we are powerful beyond measure. It is our light, not our darkness that
most frightens us. We ask ourselves, who am I to be brilliant, gorgeous,
talented, fabulous? Actually, who are you not to be?"

— MARIANNE WILLIAMSON

HAVE YOU EVER WATCHED CHILDREN PLAYING
and said, "I wish I had some of that energy?" Just this morning,
I watched two of my children run down the sidewalk while we
were out for a walk. No reason, they just ran. They ran for the
simple joy of running.

My son found a puddle in the sidewalk. He stopped right in
the middle of it and stomped his foot down, splashing muddy
water all over. He laughed joyfully and did it several more times.
Then he remembered his sister who was up ahead and ran after
her.

You were probably alive and energetic like that when you
were a kid. What happened? Where did that energy go?

Performers, artists, and athletes are very much alive when
they are performing. A great performance requires lots of energy. The energy they access and share is part of what makes
them so great, so much larger than life.

We want to be alive like them, so we emulate performers and athletes. Money is part of it. Most of us would like to be rich and famous. And yet it's much more than the money and fame we want.

We want their energy, the life force flowing through them. We are naturally drawn to that energy. It's the energy of life itself, and it carries with it the passion and vitality we long to experience.

Children are so alive and energetic because they don't hold back. They haven't learned to suppress themselves. They haven't started to limit and control their life force. They haven't learned the rules that dictate who and what they can be. And so, they're just being who they are and responding to life.

This makes them the very essence of life, fully engaged with everything around them. Life is moment to moment, fun and exciting.

Have you stopped living with the energy and passion of a child? When did that happen? And why?

Children take what life offers and roll with it. They play all day long. They play until they can't play any longer, right up until the moment they nod off to sleep. Life is one great and exciting adventure, and they are naturally driven to explore every moment.

Artists and athletes access a similar energy. Think of a great performer. What is it that makes them great?

Artists and athletes are playing. They're great because they access the same source that makes children so energetic. They are fully engaged as life, with life. They are passionately alive, like children, when they're performing.

Listen to what many top athletes say before a big game. They'll say that they just need to relax and have fun. When they're having fun, they perform well. They perform well because they're out there being instead of trying to make something happen. They're going with the flow, not trying to limit and control what is happening.

Great artists and performers find a way to allow the creative energy of life to flow through them. That is what you feel in a great work of art or a magnificent performance. It is the creative power of life that you feel and respond to. It's not the artist you are moved by. The artist is the tool. It's the energy of life that wields the tool that moves you. It reminds you that you, too, are filled with life.

Great artists and performers allow the creative energy of life to move them and move through them. They contact the energy of the divine, and that is what makes them great.

It calls to your spirit. You respond and feel wonderful as a result.

What is it that stops you from being like a great athlete or performer? What do they have that you lack?

Something amazing happens when an artist, athlete, or performer contacts the source of their strength and inspiration. They get in touch with the limitless source of life energy and inspiration that is never-ending. It comes from the divine and guides them in what they do. As a result, they are able to channel and express the brilliance and creative power of the divine and bring it to life through what they do.

It's not the human being; it is life itself. It is the energy of the divine flowing through the artist or performer that makes them great.

That very same energy and brilliance is available to you.

It's not what you do, it's who you are. When you're focused on trying to do something or make something happen, you lose touch with your innate brilliance. If you can stay focused on who you are, your inner light will shine through and your work will be an expression of your brilliance.

Maybe you haven't known what it is or how to get in touch with it. Maybe you think that famous people were given something you don't have.

It's easy to forget they are no different than you. You came from the same place and will return to the same place. Your spirit is the same as their spirit. All you need to do is open to it and allow it to move through you.

It's only you that stops you from expressing your divine brilliance.

You can be great. Or, more accurately, you are great. It's just that you've stopped it from reaching the surface. Look inward. Open to your own inner brilliance and the energy of life that flows through you. Step out of the way and allow it to guide and direct everything you do. Be great and timeless, passionately alive and energetic.

There is a well-known saying: "Ask and it will be made available to you." Or, as I once heard a motivational speaker say: "They that ask, get!"

The point is, you must ask, and you have to do your part.

All great artists, athletes, and performers work very hard to get where they are. They do their part and put in the time. They don't wake up one day and create great things. They don't go from couch potato to world record holder overnight. They have to train and be almost single-minded in their focus and devotion to their art or sport.

You must be willing to put in the work. You must choose to stay present and engaged with life no matter what obstacles appear. You must avoid the temptation to limit your Self or turn away in fear.

In every situation, in each moment, you can say yes or you can say no. The choice is yours. It's not about the outside. It's about the inside. It's not about what's going on around you. It's how you respond. It's the essence of what we call free will.

The creator has given you everything you need. You have all the energy, wisdom, and brilliance you could ever want. It's alive inside of you. It is you. You are the brilliance and energy you seek.

Start today. Make a firm commitment to be your Self and be great. Don't settle for the mediocrity of normalcy. You are better—much better—than that.

You're not here to be small and insignificant, dull and lifeless. You're here to be the light of the divine, living in physical human form. Live that truth and the energy you had as a kid will return. The truth is it never left. You just turned away.

Your body might change but you don't. You're exactly the same as you were the day you were born.

Children haven't learned to be old and tired. Children have not started to exhaust themselves worrying about all the things they cannot control. They haven't learned to watch the clock, thinking about past and future. They simply live.

Great athletes and performers do something similar. They move from thinking into being. Great performances don't come from thinking, they come from the creative energy of spiritual presence.

Athletes talk about the point at which the game "slowed down" for them. It's the point at which their greatness became apparent. They were good before. But now they're suddenly amazing.

Time doesn't change. It's the athletes who change. They change on the inside where it matters most. They stop thinking and start being.

This amazing change comes from making a shift in perception or awareness. They move from being limited by time to being timeless. Once they're timeless, the game slows down. They start living and responding from a state of consciousness that is uncoupled from the limitations of time.

I had a powerful experience of this phenomenon during a crash in a bicycle race. Many people who have had an accident or lived through a traumatic event have experienced something similar. Like the athlete for whom the game magically slows down, time slowed down for me.

Thinking back, I remember amazing details, too many to fit the moment. It was like I was watching a movie of the crash.

If you've ever had a serious accident, you probably know what I'm talking about. Time slows. The moment becomes minutes. You become aware of amazing details, things most people miss.

During my race, we rounded a corner single file, going very fast. The road narrowed to accommodate a median running down the middle of the next street. Unfortunately, the rider in front of me misjudged and hit the median. He was on his bike one moment and sprawled on the pavement the next. His small error created big, big changes in the race.

We fell like dominoes. One rider crashed over another until there was enough separation to allow someone to maneuver around the mayhem and stop the chain of crashing bicycles.

In real time, the crash lasted seconds. In my memory, it was far longer. How does this happen?

The perception of life slowing down does not happen because the clock moves slower. The clock doesn't change: you do. You access a different state of consciousness. In that other-than-conscious state, your awareness of time is forgotten. For that moment, time stops.

You move from being dominated by thought to being present. You move into simple awareness. In your altered state of consciousness, time passes differently and may not pass at all.

A serious accident shocks you out of thinking. When thinking stops, time stops. Time is a product of your mind. So when you move away from the thoughts of your mind, time ceases to exist. In that state, everything changes and you become aware of the things that truly matter.

This altered state of consciousness is always available to you. You don't have to be in a serious accident. You can choose to be fully present any time you want.

You can experience timelessness. It's created by placing your awareness on your Self and the moment. Let everything else fade into the background. You've created the distractions that keep you from being present. You can just as easily let them disappear. As a spiritual being, you're not defined, limited, or imprisoned by time. You are timeless.

The truth of timelessness is experienced in the unusual and extraordinary. You probably think of them as miracles. But they are anything but miracles; they're simply the way it is.

The problem is that you believe in time more than you believe in your own spiritual timelessness. The strength of your belief stops you from being the great and timeless being you were created to be.

The divine didn't create you to be small and insignificant, dull and lifeless. You were created to be big, bold, and amazing. All you have to do is turn away from your thoughts and toward your true Self. When you do, your life will become extraordinary just as it is meant to be.

BE YOUR SELF AND BE WELL!

❧ HEALING EXERCISE

Be Great and Timeless

Find a quiet place to sit where you can be comfortable and undistracted.

Breathe slowly, deeply, and rhythmically, following the air as it moves in and out of your body. Breathe until you feel calm, relaxed, and centered within your Self.

Notice how you feel in your chest and belly. Notice that you don't have to do anything to feel wonderful, content, and alive. Those things are part of your being, unrelated to doing.

Ask your Self this yes-or-no question: As a spiritual being, am I limited by time?

Next, say, "I am great and timeless. I have something invaluable to share. It is my true Self. The creator made me to be me. Being me is my life's purpose."

Continue to breathe deeply and allow your Self to resonate with those statements. Allow your Self to feel the strength and energy of your inner truth.

Do some writing or journaling about your experience.

CHAPTER EIGHTEEN

YOU HAVE EVERYTHING YOU NEED

"Everything in the universe is within you. Ask all from yourself."

— RUMI

"THE LORD IS MY SHEPHERD; I SHALL NOT WANT."

I speak this Psalm 23 Bible verse every morning. For me, it is the simple truth. The Lord is my shepherd. And, because of that, I do have all I need. It can't be any other way.

This one deceptively simple statement changes everything. It changes the way I think and feel. It completely changes the way I see the world around me.

I see the world with eyes that truly appreciate all I have been given. The situations and circumstances of my life don't change this. No matter what might be happening, I have all I need. The same is true for you.

You might ask your Self, "As a spiritual being, what do I lack?" When I ask my Self this question, the answer I always get is "nothing."

When you are aware of who you are and where you came from, there will be no doubt that you have everything you need. Your spirit knows no wanting. As a creation of the divine you are whole and complete.

Wanting is a product of your mind. It comes from your ego's perception of lack. Your ego wants endlessly because its wants are never satisfied. If you listen to your ego, you will always find your Self wanting. Your mind only focuses on what it believes it doesn't have.

On the other hand, your true Self, created in the image of the divine, is content and satisfied. Place your attention here.

Turn your attention away from the thoughts of your mind and toward the acceptance of your true Self and you will be content.

Everything that happens, happens for a reason. All things follow the creator's design. And, as part of that design, all things work together for good. The situations of your life and the circumstances you find your Self in are all happening for a divinely guided reason. In some way, they are just what you need.

The creator is in charge and provides even when you can't see or understand it. Your job is to stay present and look for the deeper meaning in all things. This is true even when you can't see or understand. Don't mistake your own limited awareness to mean the creator is absent.

If you prayed with only one statement, the opening line of Psalm 23 is a great choice. It says everything that needs to be said.

Surrender your human desire for control. Acknowledge that the divine is in charge. There isn't anything you need to worry about. Everything is as it should be.

You are a creation of the divine. You have been created in the image of the creator who is perfection. There is nothing you lack, need, or want.

Everything you experience in this world is nothing more than things that are happening around you. Nothing touches you directly. You have a physical human body, but that body is not who you are. You're not physical, you're spiritual.

You live and love. You learn. You experience this physical, material world. When you're done, you return home to the creator. It is where you came from, and it is where you will return.

Knowing these things in your heart and soul allows you to relax like never before. Nothing is as significant as your ego or thinking mind makes it out to be. Worrying is unnecessary and pointless. Unless, of course, you want to suffer.

This life is very much like a playground. It's a physical playground for spiritual beings. You can relax and play. It's an important part of why you're here.

You're not here to live in fear and constant worry, trying to control everything. You're here to be you and enjoy the experience to the best of your ability.

When you relax and accept this as the truth, everything will flow more smoothly. You will encounter fewer problems. You'll worry far less. You'll be able to remain calm even in outward chaos. Joy and contentment will be yours.

There might be lack in the physical world. There might be things you think you want and need. But they will often be, upon deeper exploration, things that satisfy material desires. They're not the things of spirit that feed and satisfy the real you. Try to avoid the temptation of mistaking physical, material lack as something you lack.

If you can stay present and aware, you will grow stronger in your presence as a spiritual being. It will gradually become as clear and certain as the blue sky on a sunny day, undeniable.

Nothing in the physical world defines you in any way. You are far more than the physical form you see and touch, your body that lives and dies. You are the inner spirit that animates your physical form. You are timeless and eternal.

You are the primary entity. The body you inhabit, with all of its physical needs and requirements, is secondary to you in every way. And you are the foundation upon which the health and well-being of your body is built.

Spirituality is the food you eat and the air you breathe. Spirituality is the source of your health and well-being. If you're not fully present, your body simply won't have the energy it needs to be healthy.

You are the life force, the energy of life itself. Your body needs you to live and be well. Restricting and limiting your Self is where sickness and decline begin.

When you're not present as your true Self, the voice in your head takes over and replaces you. You'll start to live and act from your thoughts instead of your Self. This is when you become negative and judgmental.

When you believe the voice in your head, you'll move into shame and guilt, fear and anxiety. Believing the voice of your ego is what creates your suffering.

If you find your Self being negative and judgmental, or feeling worried, you can be certain you're acting from your ego and not your true Self. It's time to return your focus to spirit. Hit the reset button and start over.

Fear, anxiety, and shame are all emotional reactions to believing you are something you are not.

The voice in your head might say something like, "I am ugly or unattractive." The truth is that you are a beautiful creation of the divine.

The voice in your head might say, "I am stupid." The truth is that the creator has blessed you with great wisdom.

Even sickness can be used as a Self-judgment. You are not sick. You are never sick. You can't be sick because you're not a physical being. You are always the same: strong, healthy, perfect.

When you live as your true Self instead of your thoughts,

your perception of everything will change for the better. You will live as the life and love you are. Everyone and everything around you will respond to the real you. You will find your Self living a life that mirrors who you are, a creation of the divine.

Look for the light of the divine in all things, especially your Self. When things appear to be bad and unworkable, when you're sick and in pain, when there is no love to be found, remember they are physical and superficial. Underneath, the light of the divine is there.

Allow the inspiration and guidance that comes from the creator to speak to you. New solutions will arise. Your awareness of love will return. The sickness will pass. You are whole and have everything you need. It's right there inside of you.

BE YOUR SELF AND BE WELL!

|||||||||||||||||||||||||||||||||||||||||||||||||||||||||||||||||||||||||||||||||||||||||

❧ HEALING EXERCISE

You Have Everything You Need

Find a quiet place where you can sit comfortably and be undistracted.

If moving helps you feel present and meditative, you can do the exercise while walking.

If you choose to try the walking method, be aware that you'll need to walk very slowly and with no particular destination. It's also best to walk in a quiet place in nature. Nature provides the energy of thoughtless presence, which can help strengthen your presence.

Breathe slowly, rhythmically, and deeply. You can breathe

in and out through your nose, or you can breathe in through your nose and out through your mouth. Choose whichever feels right. There is no "wrong" way.

As you breathe, focus your attention on your chest and belly. Feel your chest and belly rise as you breathe in. Let them relax and fall as you breathe out.

Allow your awareness to be centered in your chest and belly.

If you have thoughts that creep in, just notice them and continue breathing. Return your focus to your chest and belly without resisting the thoughts. Acknowledge them and move on. Resisting your thoughts will only strengthen them.

Notice the subtle sensations in your chest and belly. Allow your Self to be calm, present, and centered within your Self.

When you feel ready, ask the following yes-or-no questions:

As a spiritual being, do I have everything I need?

Does any situation or circumstance in this life have the power to touch or limit my true Self?

Allow your Self to respond with a simple yes or no. Don't give in to the temptation to ask "why" or define it any further. Those things come from your thoughts. If you follow, you'll get lost and confused.

Simply accept your answer and sit in the energy of your awareness.

Do some writing or journaling about your experience. Make note of how your awareness might influence you in your daily life.

DAILY AFFIRMATIONS

I REPEAT THESE AFFIRMATIONS EVERY DAY. THEY help me stay focused on who and what I am. They strengthen my presence and help me stay focused on my divine mission in life.

I suggest making them a part of your daily practice. They are reminders about who and what you are. The more you say them, the stronger they will become. The truth will solidify and grow inside of you. Use those that speak to you. Add words you resonate with. Incorporate other affirmations and prayers. Make it something that is yours and works for you.

I am a spiritual being created in the image of the divine.
I am spirit.

I was made by love, as love, and for love. Love is who I am
and why I am here.

I have a human body. It is wonderful and amazing,
a living house for my spirit.

I love my body. But it doesn't define me in any way.

I am the inside, not the outside.

I am the inner spirit that animates my body and makes it
a living organism.

Without me and my life force, my body would die.

I am here to be my Self.

I am here to share my voice and my innate wisdom with the world.

The creator made me to be me. Being me is my life's purpose.

I give my Self over to this mission today and every day.

I choose to live as my true Self.

ACTIVITIES THAT SUPPORT HEALING

THE FOLLOWING IS A LIST OF THINGS YOU CAN consider incorporating into your daily life to assist you in achieving your healing goals. You don't have to do them all. You don't even have to do any of them. But healing is a process and a journey. It is a lifelong unfolding that requires practice and commitment. The more you put in, the more you get out. These exercises represent an outward expression of the inner commitment you have made to grow and heal. The divine responds to those who step up and ask. These activities are ways you can speak up and make your intentions known.

Walk

Walk in nature as often as possible. No headphones. No talking. Walk and listen. Pay attention to your body and the world around you. Notice the sights, sounds, and smells. Feel the air. Feel the sun. See the sky. Try to observe without thinking and analyzing. Just be with your body and the natural world.

Breathe

Sit and breathe deeply, slowly, and rhythmically. Do this daily, even multiple times a day. Breathe until you feel a sense of inner calm.

Listen

Listen to the sounds of nature. Listen to the birds and animals. Listen to the insects. Listen to the sounds of your house. Listen to others with no thought about how to respond. Just listen to get to know them.

Pray

Live your life as if every breath and every word is a prayer. Pray gratitude. Pray joy and contentment. Pray words that affirm the truth about who and what you are as a creation of the divine. "I am" is a great way to start any prayer.

Meditate

Meditation is similar to praying, breathing, and listening. It incorporates aspects of all three. Meditation is purposeful quiet, quiet that allows you to hear your inner voice. There is a common misperception that if you are meditating correctly, your mind will be still and quiet. That will almost never happen. Trying to make your mind be completely quiet will only lead to frustration. The more you try to make it stop, the more it will talk. The trick is to acknowledge and accept this. Forget trying to stop your mind from talking. Instead, turn your attention away from your mind and to your chest and belly. Listen to how you feel instead of listening to the words in your head.

Read

Read books of substance and meaning. Read the works of authors you resonate with, heart and soul. Read books that make your heart sing and your soul come to life.

Choose Quiet

Quiet is a rare commodity in our world. You must be committed and purposeful about it. Turn off the noise-makers. Turn off the radio, television, computer, phone, iPod, iPad, Kindle, and any other noise-makers you might have. At first, it might make you crazy. You might even go through cravings or signs of addiction. These things will pass. Eventually, if you stay with it, you will begin to crave quiet.

Yoga

Yoga is a great tool for using your body to enhance your spiritual presence. Choose a class that moves slowly and is not rushed. Many classes are overly focused on the body. They neglect the spirit. Choose a class that acknowledges that yoga is a blending of mind, body, and spirit. It's not just exercise. It's mindful, soulful presence.

Slow Down

We live in a frantic, busy world. The pace of life today is incompatible with the presence and awareness you need to heal. Slow it down. Look for things you can cut from your schedule. Doing stops being. Look for ways to disconnect from the clock. Every moment spent unaware of what time it is, is a moment of freedom.

Look Inward

Instead of looking around to decide what to do, look inward. Ask your Self what you want to do. Ask your Self where you want to be. Ask about every choice and every decision. Does this support and enhance the real me? Or will it be a distraction that limits my healing?

Be in Nature

Take every opportunity to get outside. If possible, make time to be in the natural world. Go to a park. Find a path through the woods. Sit by a lake or river. If you're fortunate enough to have access to a wilderness area, go there as often as you can. Just get outside and immerse your Self in the simple rhythm of life.

Eat

Eat good food. Eat only the best, the food that makes your body vibrantly healthy and alive. Eat every color, the more the better. Color is life. If there are foods that make your body feel bad, don't eat them. Your body is telling you how it feels about that food. Don't ignore the message. Eat to live instead of living to eat. Slow down and be with your food. Smell it. Look at it. Savor it. Ask your Self if the food you are going to eat supports the life and health of your body. If it does, eat freely. If it doesn't, limit it or don't eat it.

Move

Move your body. Your body craves movement. Do it with the intention of using body movement to get in touch with your Self. No headphones or television; they're a distraction. Move to get in touch with your body. Start moving and then pay attention to your feet. Notice how they feel. Next, pay attention to your lower legs. Notice how they feel. Move up through your body, pausing at each body part to check in. If there is a part of your body that has pain, concentrate on that part longer. See if you can get a feel for what that body part might be saying or what it might need.

Write

Make time for writing or journaling. I suggest making it a daily practice. It is a way to bring your experiences into concrete form. It is also a way to contact your deeper wisdom and inner awareness. Things will come out in your writing that aren't clear in your thoughts. Over time, you will start to notice things and patterns that are important. You will even discover things about your Self that you didn't know before.

Stop

Stop everything that doesn't support you and your healing. Stop believing the old stories you tell your Self about who you are and what you can be. Stop saying things that are not true. Stop living for tomorrow. Stop living in fear. Stop trying to be anything other than a beautiful and beloved creation of the divine.

Start

Start living freely, fully, and passionately. Start telling your Self and others exactly who and what you are. Start speaking the truth. Say what you mean and mean what you say. Start living as if today is the only day you have. Be here now. Start living openly and fearlessly. Start living every breath, every step, and every word as your true Self. Commit to you every moment of every day for the rest of your life.

ABOUT THE AUTHOR

Steven Hiebert is a gifted healer, doctor of chiropractic, teacher, and author who lives and works in Saint Paul, Minnesota. He is deeply spiritual and believes that spirituality is an integral part of health and wellbeing. Steven's life's work and passion is helping people heal. He has been in private practice since 1990, touching countless lives.